I Am He Who Sees

Justice Defined by the Hand of God

Arthur Garrison

Keledei
PUBLICATIONS

An Imprint of Sulis International Press
Los Angeles | Dallas | London

I AM HE WHO SEES: JUSTICE DEFINED BY THE HAND OF GOD.
Copyright ©2023 by Arthur Garrison. All rights reserved.

ISBN: 978-1-958139-21-9
Published by Keledei Publications
An Imprint of Sulis International
Los Angeles | Dallas | London

www.sulisinternational.com

Contents

Introduction

> *But let justice run down like water, and right-*
> *eousness like a mighty stream.*[1]

Fīat jūstitia ruat caeum. "Let justice be done though the heavens fall," the Latin phrase proclaims. As Lord Chief Justice Hewart wrote regarding the nature of justice, "It is not merely of some importance but is of fundamental importance that justice should not only be done but should manifestly and undoubtedly be seen to be done."[2] It is innate in human nature to seek justice. But why?

In how many movies have we seen a character who was told that the evil character had suffered some type of setback and the character responds, "This is the first time I have believed there is a God!" What is the connection? Why was the suffering of the evil character an example of the existence of God?

The reason starts with what is innate in us. From early childhood through the end of life, we all have a need to see and experience fairness. How many times have we watched very small children play a game, and one says, "That's not fair?" Consider the expression of people who say to another person who has done wrong, "You know you will burn in

---

[1] Amos 5:24
[2] *Rex v. Sussex* Justices (1924) 1 K.B. 256, 259.

1

hell for this" or when someone who has done wrongs in life says to another who is equally bad, as a parting salutation, "See you in hell." The nature of mankind includes the belief that all wrongs and evil will be judged and punished. From birth, we all have an innate desire for a fair outcome in life.

This need is what we call justice. We all believe and need to believe that evil will not triumph and there will be recompense for doing evil. Secular or religious, the need of justice is satisfied in the belief that a "higher power" or "God" or "the universe" or "karma" will apply the higher truths of right and wrong to events of mankind, ensuring that evil does not prevail.

The academic and philosophical literature of Western-Christian thought and the Judeo-Christian biblical tradition are rich, dating back to the great minds of the Enlightenment and, before them, to the age of Greek and Roman philosophy. Both Greek and Roman philosophy have provided a foundation for defining the nature and purpose of justice in Western thought.

John Locke wrote that civilization cannot function in an environment—a state of nature—in which the ability of the individual to enjoy life is limited to the ability to defend life and property against theft and violence from other people. Thomas Hobbes called this state of nature "solitary, poor, nasty, brutish, and short." To avoid this state, man uses reason to define the distinction between right and wrong, which is enforced by government and positive law.

In the Christian philosophical legal tradition, Saint Thomas Aquinas wrote that there are four types of law.[3] The first is *eternal law,* which refers to the laws God established to hold the universe and all within it together. Gravity, for example, is an eternal law. *Divine law* includes the laws God dictates to mankind to govern human behavior. The Ten Commandments, for example, are part of divine law. *Natural law* is human understanding of those divine laws. Higher

---

[3]   Saint Thomas Aquinas, Richard J. Regan, and William P. Baumgarth, *On Law, Morality and Politics*, second edition (2002) at 10, 16–24.

concepts of right and wrong and morality are derived and created under natural law. From natural law, man derives moral philosophy, which includes definitions of just outcomes. The last type of law is *positive law*, which is written laws (statutes) that govern specific behavior and the application of punishments for breaking statutory laws. Laws defining homicide or burglary or speeding in a residential street are positive laws.

From the perspective of the Christian philosophical tradition, God is the source of all law and its application, which is justice. Under the eyes of God in heaven, all is seen. In the movie *Rob Roy*, a manipulative lord was told, "Do not think that all sins go unpunished in this life, Montrose."[4] God is *Adonai El Roi*, which means, the God who sees me.[5] Under divine law, God sees and defines evil and punishes it. Justice is defined and conceptualized in the belief that God is the judge of human behavior, and He responds to evil done.

Throughout the development of political, social, economic, philosophical, and religious literature over the centuries, justice has been defined in various ways. It has been defined as a process as well as an outcome. The defining of justice necessarily requires defining the meaning and purpose of law.

Although both concepts are similar in scope, they are different in both purpose and operation. The law is defined by what it does and what it requires, while justice is defined in normative terms. Justice, in normative terms, is defined by what ought to be or what should happen—whether the result is fair. Justice defined this way involves what we as a society or an individual feels *should* be the result. It's outcome

---

[4]   *Rob Roy*, directed by Michael Caton-Jones, written by Alan Sharp, featuring Liam Neeson, Jessica Lange, and John Hurt (Los Angeles: United Artists, 1995).

[5]   See the story of Hagar who said, "And she called the name of the Lord that spake unto her, Thou God seest me: for she said, Have I also here looked after him that seeth me?" (Genesis 16:13 KJV).

based. Justice can also be defined by what the law requires and whether the law is obeyed. The distinction between the operation and implementation of the two concepts involves the fact that what is required by the law is not always just, and that what is immoral is not always illegal.

The distinction between the normative (ought) and positive (legally required) perceptions of justice were debated in the 1960 movie *Exodus*. The character Ari Ben Canaan, a senior operative of the Haganah, debates the differing approaches to forcing the British out of Palestine in order to form the state of Israel with his uncle Akiva, who is the head of the Irgun.

The movie portrays the difference between the two organizations in that the Irgun utilizes acts of violence and bombing, while the Haganah uses diplomacy to achieve their shared goal.[6] In their meeting, their debate shifts from tactics to whether the Jews receiving Palestine would be a just result:

> ***Ari.*** *I think these bombings and these killings hurt us with the United Nations. A year ago, we had the respect of the whole world. Now, when they read about us, it's nothing but terror and violence.*
>
> ***Akiva.*** *It's not the first time this happens in history. I don't know of one nation, whether existing now*

---

6 For discussion on the history of these two Jewish resistance (terrorist) organizations, see generally Donald Neff, *Hamas: A Pale Image of the Jewish Irgun and Lehi Gangs*, Washington Rep. on Middle E. Aff., May/June 2006; Arthur H. Garrison, *Defining Terrorism: Philosophy of the Bomb, Propaganda by Deed and Change Through Fear and Violence*, 17 Crim. Just. Stud. 259 (2004); Arthur H. Garrison, *Terrorism: The Nature of Its History*, 16 Crim. Just. Stud. 39 (2003); David A. Charters, *Eyes of the Underground: Jewish Insurgent Intelligence in Palestine, 1945–47*, 13 Intelligence and Nat'l Security 163 (1998); James L. Fields, *Irgun Zvai Leumi: The Jewish Terrorist Element of the Arab-Israeli Conflict* (Apr. 1985) (unpublished Master's Thesis, Air Command and Staff College); Stefan Korbonski, *Unknown Chapter in the Life of Menachem Begin and Irgun Zvai Leumi*, 13 E. European Q. 373 (1979).

or in the past, that was not born in violence. Terror, violence, death. They are the midwives who bring free nations into this world and compromisers like the Haganah produce only abortions.

. . . .

***Ari.** How can we ask the UN for a just decision when we keep on blowing up things like a bunch of anarchists!*

***Akiva.** You have just used the words "a just decision." May I tell you something? Firstly, justice itself is an abstraction. Completely devoid of reality. Secondly, to speak of justice and Jews in the same breath is a logical absurdity. Thirdly, one can argue the justice of Arab claims on Palestine just as one can argue the justice of Jewish claims. Fourthly, no one can say the Jews have not had more than their share of injustice these past ten years. I therefore say, fifthly, let the next injustice work against somebody else for a change.*[7]

Akiva asserts that justice, as a concept, has no real meaning outside of personal perspective. In other words, justice is a subjective and individual concept. Is Akiva correct that justice does not have an objective or intrinsic meaning, but rather justice and injustice are defined by who wins and who loses? Is Akiva right that justice is nothing but an abstraction? Is there an objective meaning of justice by which all results are measured?

This book[8] proposes that justice is defined by who God is and what God does and why God does what He does. Jus-

---

[7] *Exodus*, directed by Otto Preminger, written by Dalton Trumbo, novel by Leon Uris, featuring Paul Newman (Otto Preminger Films,1960).

[8] Material in this book includes previously published research from my article "*Defining the Meaning and Purpose of Justice, Law, and Criminal Justice: A Hermeneutical Judeo-Christian Biblical Perspective*" 55 Journal of Catholic Legal Studies (2016): 1–86.

tice, the Scriptures tell us, is in the eyes of God, and His hand will apply justice and the weak will be defended.

But justice in the hand of God raises a separate question—what is justice in the eyes of God? It is proposed in this book that the utilization of a literal, historical, and contextual hermeneutical review of the Bible itself answers the question of what is justice in the hand of God. Justice includes the proposition that God is involved in the affairs of mankind. Justice, as the Scriptures tell us, occurs through the interaction of her three daughters–law, mercy, and grace. The approach taken in this book is that the Bible is true[9] and can be used as an exclusive authoritative source for determining the definition, purpose, and operation of justice and law.

It is asserted in this book that the text of the Bible itself provides a framework for defining the concepts of law and justice and the purpose of both. It is proposed that both law and justice have distinctive meanings; the source of both can be defined by the nature of God, as reflected in the Bible.[10]

Because the Bible is the result of divine revelation, it can be sought for answers to practical problems.[11] Taking the

---

[9] The Bible is the inspired word of God, "For we did not follow cunningly devised fables when we made known to you … Jesus Christ, but were eyewitnesses of His majesty. For He received from God the Father honor and glory… And we heard this voice which came from heaven when we were with Him on the holy mountain. And so we have the prophetic word confirmed…knowing…Scripture… never came by the will of man, but holy men of God spoke as they were moved by the Holy Spirit." (2 Peter 1:16–21). See also 2 Timothy 3:16–17; 2 Samuel 23:22; Jeremiah 1:7, 9; Exodus 4:14–15; Isaiah 51:16; Deuteronomy 18:18; 2 Peter 3:15–16.

[10] For discussion on the hermeneutical proof and utility of the Bible, see, Arthur H. Garrison, *A Hermeneutical Proof of the Bible. Journal of Grace Theology*, 5(1):3–38 (2018).

[11] See 2 Timothy 3:16–17 ("All Scripture is given by inspiration of God, and is profitable for doctrine, for reproof, for correction, for instruction in righteousness, that the man of God may be complete, thoroughly equipped for every good work." See also Proverbs 2:6–7 ("For the Lord gives wisdom; from His mouth come knowledge and understanding; He stores up sound wisdom for the upright") and Proverbs 1:4 ("To give prudence to the simple, to the young man knowledge and discretion—").

Bible as authoritative, this book examines whether the Bible provides a workable definition and conception of justice outside of personal subjective experience. Put another way, starting the inquiry from the proposition that there is a God and that the Bible is His word to mankind, can objective scholarly review of the text provide an answer to the inquiry of what is justice? This book proposes that the answer to the question can be provided in the affirmative.

1.
Do Justly, Love Mercy, and Walk Humbly with Your God[1]

While there is much debate on the meaning of justice and law, both in academic[2] and legal[3] scholarship, there are questions that precedes defining what is justice. Why is justice sought by mankind in the first place? Why is justice valued over evil or injustice? What principle is vindicated by the demand and achievement of justice?

The principle vindicated by justice is the priority of right over wrong, good over evil. It is this principle—that by God's word[4]—objective right and wrong are defined, as well as the edict that evil should not prevail—that supports the demand for justice. But this truth leads to another question: what is right and wrong? What is the source of defining these two ideas? It is at this level of conceptualization of justice that the Judeo-Christian biblical tradition has formed the foundation for legal Western thought.

---

[1] Micah 6:8.

[2] Arthur H. Garrison, *The Traditions and History of the Meaning of the Rule of Law*, 12 Geo. J.L. & Pub. Pol'y 565, 565 (2014).

[3] Arthur H. Garrison, *The Rule of Law and the Rise of Control of Executive Power*, 18 Tex. Rev. of L. & Pol. 303, 304 (2014).

[4] For example, see Leviticus 18; Deuteronomy 18:9–14; Leviticus 20:6; Isaiah 8:19; Leviticus 19: 31 ("Give no regard to mediums and familiar spirits; do not seek after them, to be defiled by them: I am the Lord your God.").

A. For the Lord is a God of justice,[5] the Almighty will not pervert justice,[6] and the judgments of the Lord are true and righteous altogether[7]

The Judeo-Christian biblical tradition begins with doctrinal assertions that there is a God.[8] A tradition that asserts that God is just, but also, He is the source of the meaning of justice. As Isaiah explained, "Therefore the Lord will wait, that He may be gracious to you; and therefore He will be exalted, that He may have mercy on you. For the Lord is a God of justice; blessed are all those who wait for Him."[9] King David, when reflecting on the nature of God, wrote, "[T]he Lord abides forever; He has established His throne for judgment, and He will judge the world in righteousness; He will execute judgment for the peoples with equity."[10]

Christian tradition makes clear that there will be a day when all that has been done will be judged and evil will not go unpunished:

> And I saw the dead, the great, and the small, standing before the throne, and books were opened; and another book was opened, which is the book of life; and the dead were judged from the things which were written in the books, according to their deeds. And the sea gave up the dead which were in it, and death and Hades gave up the dead which were in them, and they were judged, every one of them according to their deeds.[11]

---

[5] Isaiah 30:18.
[6] Job 34:12.
[7] Psalm 19:9.
[8] Isaiah 44:6 ("Thus says the Lord, the King of Israel, and his Redeemer, the Lord of hosts: I am the First and I am the Last; besides Me there is no God.").
[9] Isaiah 30:18.
[10] Psalms 9:7–8 (NASB1995).
[11] Revelation 20:12–13 (NASB1995).

One of the aspects of justice in the Christian tradition is that the sins of men don't escape the eyes of God, and there will be a day when each person will account for evil done. Justice is defined by the fact that there will be an accounting. As Paul wrote regarding those who judge the actions of men and those who do evil and know their actions to be evil,

> *the judgment of God is according to truth . . . And do you think this, O man, you who judge those practicing such things, and doing the same, that you will escape the judgment of God?*[12]

Paul's point is that judges will be judged by what they do and how they judge. Jesus said, "For with what judgment you judge, you will be judged; and with the measure you use, it will be measured back to you."[13] God instructed Moses to tell the judges of Israel that they were to judge equally between bother and stranger and not to use unequal scales in judgment.[14] As David wrote, "Your law is truth."[15]

But in the same admonition, Paul explains that God's justice and judgment, although inevitable, includes His mercy and providing those who do evil the opportunity to recognize it and repent.

> *Or do you despise the riches of His goodness, forbearance, and long-suffering, not knowing that the goodness of God leads you to repentance? But in accordance with your hardness and your impenitent heart, you are treasuring up for yourself wrath in the day of wrath and revelation of the righteous judgment of God, who "will render to each one according to his deeds". . . To those who are self-seeking and do not obey the truth, but obey unright-*

---

[12] Romans 2:2–3.
[13] Matthew 7:2.
[14] Leviticus 19:15, 35; Deuteronomy 16:18–20. See also Proverbs 20:23.
[15] Psalm 119:142.

*eousness—indignation and wrath, tribulation and
anguish, on every soul of man who does evil.[16]*

Paul explained that the patience of justice should not be despised but accepted. The patience of justice should not be confused with indulgence or indifference to evil.

For "[r]ighteousness and justice are the foundation of Your throne; mercy and truth go before Your face."[17] Justice is defined by first recognizing the promise of God—that all is seen and recorded by God, and all actions are measured by His law of right and wrong. There will be an accounting of all men for their actions. "For he who does wrong will receive the consequences of the wrong which he has done, and that without partiality."[18]

Justice flows from the existence of God Himself. Justice has a standard. It is an objective standard. Not only is God a God of justice, but justice is defined by what God does, how He does it, and why He does it.

God's justice is defined by how His courts worked during the first recorded crimes in the history of the universe.

The first crimes of the universe did not occur in the Garden of Eden. They occurred in the throne room of heaven itself, when Satan committed sedition and armed rebellion, resulting in his ejection from heaven and from his status as an archangel. When expelled from heaven, Satan committed additional crimes that engulfed Adam and Eve. Through the resulting criminal trials, the justice of God made its entrance into the nature of things in heaven and on earth.

---

[16] Romans 2:4–6, 8–9.
[17] Psalm 89:14.
[18] Colossians 3:25 (NASB); see also 2 Thessalonians 1:8–10 (NKJV) ("[D]ealing out retribution to those who do not know God and to those who do not obey the gospel of our Lord Jesus. These will pay the penalty of eternal destruction, away from the presence of the Lord and from the glory of His power.").

"In the beginning," we are told, "God created the heavens and the earth."[19] He created "the heavens . . . all His angels . . . all His hosts . . . all stars of light . . . the heavens of heavens . . . the waters above the heavens! . . . He commanded and they were created. He has also established them forever and ever; He made a decree which shall not pass away. . . . His name alone is exalted; His glory is above the earth and heaven."[20]

God Himself defended the exclusivity and majesty of His work when He commanded Job to explain how creation functioned.[21] When He gave the Ten Commandments to the children of Israel, He Himself declared that He "the Lord made the heavens and the earth, the sea, and all that is in them."[22] God made clear through His prophets that He is God, and said, "My glory I do not grant to another."[23] Which brings us to the story of Satan.

When God created the heavens, He created angels by the thousands upon thousands without number,[24] and among them was Lucifer. Lucifer was an archangel who was in charge of all music and praise before the throne of God.[25] But Lucifer grew proud and wanted to sit on the throne of God himself.[26]

The indictment against Lucifer was, "You said in your heart, 'I will ascend to the heavens; I will raise my throne above the stars of God; I will sit enthroned on the mount of assembly . . . I will ascend above the tops of the clouds; I

[19] Genesis 1:1; Colossians 1:16.
[20] Psalm 148:1–4, 13.
[21] Job 38:1–41.
[22] Exodus 20:11.
[23] Isaiah 42:8 (NCB).
[24] Daniel 7:10; Psalms 68:17; Revelation 5:11.
[25] Ezekiel 28:13–14.
[26] Ezekiel 28:17.

will make myself like the Most High.'"[27] When Lucifer acted upon his plan,

> *war broke out in heaven: Michael and his angels*
> *fought with the dragon; and the dragon and his an-*
> *gels fought, but they did not prevail, nor was a*
> *place found for them in heaven any longer. So the*
> *great dragon was cast out, that serpent of old,*
> *called the Devil and Satan, who deceives the whole*
> *world; he was cast to the earth, and his angels were*
> *cast out with him.*[28]

The first crimes in the history of existence had occurred;
they were sedition and armed rebellion.

God's judgment for the sedition and armed rebellion was
this: "I cast you as a profane thing out of the mountain of
God; and I destroyed you, O covering cherub, from the midst
of the fiery stones."[29] Lucifer was perfect from the day he
was created but he chose to do evil.[30] The indictment against
Lucifer reads that, "Your heart was lifted up because of your
beauty; You corrupted your wisdom for the sake of your
splendor."[31]

Lucifer chose to adopt pride over reverence in heaven and
God threw him out of heaven, along with one-third of the
entire number of angels in heaven who followed him.[32] Cast
down from heaven he landed on earth.

Regarding Satan's expulsion, Jesus said, "I saw Satan fall
like lightning from heaven."[33]

God Himself said, "I turned you to ashes upon the
earth."[34]

---

[27] Isaiah 14:13–14 (NIV).
[28] Revelation 12:7–9.
[29] Ezekiel 28:16.
[30] Ezekiel 28:15.
[31] Ezekiel 28:17.
[32] Revelation 12:4.
[33] Luke 10:18.
[34] Ezekiel 28:18.

Knowing God had judged Satan for sedition and that Satan had complete contempt for God and all that He made in heaven and on earth, the story of Adam and Eve has a context. God created Lucifer to serve heaven at the throne of God, and when he refused, he was dismissed from heaven by the word of God and the sword of Michael.

Then God cleaned up the damage done. God looked and saw "the earth was without form, and void; and darkness was on the face of the deep," and seeing it, God said over the next six days, "Let there be . . . and there was . . ."[35] After five days of creation by His utterance, on the sixth day, God said,

> *Let Us make man in Our image, according to Our*
> *likeness; let them have dominion over the fish of the*
> *sea, over the birds of the air, and over the cattle,*
> *over all the earth and over every creeping thing*
> *that creeps on the earth.[36]*

The context of the beginning of Genesis is that Satan had not been only thrown out of heaven and cast down to the earth, but God had repaired the damage to the "heavens and the earth" and He placed Adam and Eve over the earth to dominate and enjoy it.

Satan was having none of it, and that brings us to the story of the forbidden fruit and the trials of Adam, Eve, the serpent, and Satan.

In Genesis, God tells Adam that he has all the Garden of Eden to enjoy, and he was given the job of protecting it and growing it.[37] When God placed Adam in the perfect garden, there was one law that God required him to obey, and that

---

[35] Genesis 1:2–25.
[36] Genesis 1:26.
[37] Genesis 2:15 ("Then the Lord God took the man and put him in the garden of Edan to tend and keep it.").

law had a sanction. He told Adam, "Of every tree of the garden thou mayest freely eat: But of the tree of the knowledge
of good and evil, thou shalt not eat of it: for in the day that
thou eatest thereof thou shalt surely die."[38] Next, God created Eve,[39] and both Adam and Eve enjoyed the garden.

The garden was God's special creation for man on the
earth, and Satan wanted to destroy its perfection. Satan knew
he did not have the power to do so, but he determined that
since he could not destroy a creation of God, he would steal
control over it from Adam. So Satan developed a plan that
included a new set of crimes. His crimes started with conspiracy to commit criminal trespass. Who did he conspire
with? This is where the serpent comes into the story.

The serpent had access to the garden, and he agreed with
Satan to allow Satan to use his physical being to function in
the physical realm on the earth. Remember, Satan was a fall-
en angel, a spirit, not a physical creature. He needed a body
to speak through, to communicate with Eve. Satan picked the
serpent because the serpent "was more cunning than any
beast of the field which the Lord God had made."[40] The cunning of the serpent, as Jesus explained, was that he was
wise.[41] He was wiser than all the beasts of the field in Eden.
That is why Satan picked him. But wise as the serpent was,
he chose corruption and cooperation with Satan.

Satan and the serpent agreed to work together to get Eve to
sin. Thus, the next crime was conspiracy to commit fraud.
What fraud? They agreed to get Eve and then Adam to be-
lieve the fruit from the Tree of the Knowledge of Good and
Evil was not forbidden and would actually make them better.
Which was a lie. Fraud is knowing what you say is false and

---

[38] Genesis 2:16–17 (KJV).
[39] Genesis 2:21–22.
[40] Genesis 3:1.
[41] Matthew 10:16.

to get another to believe the lie is true, to the detriment of the person hearing the lie.[42]

The serpent said to Eve, "Ye shall not surely die: for God doth know that in the day ye eat thereof, then your eyes shall be opened, and ye shall be as gods, knowing good and evil."[43] With Adam standing there, Eve took the fruit and ate some and gave some to Adam, who also ate some of the fruit.[44]

Satan had won. God had given lease authority over the earth to Adam and Eve, and in following Satan and obeying him, they transferred the rights to control human behavior from being under God's direction and influence to being under Satan's.

This is how Satan could later tempt Jesus and say, "All this authority I will give You, and their glory; for this has been delivered to me, and I give it to whomever I wish. Therefore, if You will worship before me, all will be Yours."[45]

When Satan said all the earth was his and he could give it to whomever he wished, Jesus did not dispute the assertion that Satan had authority on earth. For that matter, Jesus confirmed it when he referred to Satan as "the ruler of this world."[46]

Adam's sin transferred the lease of the earth to Satan, but not the title. When Satan's day comes, God will regain unquestioned authority over the earth when He exercises His rights as title owner. Satan's lease will be up.

---

[42] For example see, *Bash v. Bell Telephone Co. of Pennsylvania*, 411 Pa. Super. 347, 601 A.2d 825 (1992); *Agathos v. Starlite Motel*, 60 F.3d 143, 147 (3d Cir. 1995); *Bortz v. Noon*, 556 Pa. 489, __, 729 A.2d 555, 560 (1999).

[43] Genesis 3:4–5 (KJV).

[44] Genesis 3:6.

[45] Luke 4:6–7.

[46] John 14:30. See also 2 Corinthians 4:4; Ephesians 2:2; John 12:31.

Adam and Eve broke the law of the garden, and the first criminal trial in the history of mankind occurred. When they stood before the court of God, God asked what they had done. Adam said to God, who had been looking for him, "I heard thy voice in the garden, and I was afraid because I was naked; and I hid myself."[47]

God said, "Who told thee that thou wast naked? Hast thou eaten of the tree, whereof I commanded thee that thou shouldest not eat?"[48]

Rather than face up to his sin, to use a contemporary expression, Adam threw Eve under the bus and said, "The woman whom thou gavest to be with me, she gave me of the tree, and I did eat."[49]

Eve, following Adam's example, threw the serpent under the bus. When "the Lord God said unto the woman, What is this that thou hast done? . . . the woman said, The serpent beguiled me, and I did eat."[50]

It is not recorded if the serpent said anything after receiving blame from Eve, but he very well could have pled that he had no choice but to help a former archangel.

In the first trial in the history of mankind, the defense of mitigation was utilized, and each defendant tried to transfer their responsibility by blaming their codefendant.[51]

After hearing the defenses, God found each defendant guilty and sentenced each according to their guilt. Before the court of God, justice requires the recognition of evil and the application of an appropriate sanction specific to the crime done.

The serpent was guilty of conspiracy to commit criminal trespass on the property of Eden by Satan and conspiracy to

---

[47] Genesis 3:10 (KJV).
[48] Genesis 3:11 (KJV).
[49] Genesis 3:12 (KJV).
[50] Genesis 3:13 (KJV).
[51] Genesis 3:12–13.

commit fraud. The serpent was also guilty of the crime of solicitation and facilitation to commit theft.

Criminal solicitation "is the intentional encouragement of an unlawful act"[52] and criminal facilitation "also called aiding and abetting—is the provision of assistance to a wrongdoer with the intent to further an offense's commission."[53] The "crime of solicitation is complete as soon as the encouragement occurs, liability for aiding and abetting [criminal facilitation] requires that a wrongful act be carried out. Neither solicitation nor facilitation requires lending physical aid; for both, words may be enough."[54]

The "serpent deceived Eve by his craftiness"[55] regarding what God had said and why God said it for the purpose of inducing her to take the fruit (solicitation). Asking someone to commit a specific crime is solicitation.[56]

The "serpent said to the woman, 'You will not surely die. For God knows that in the day you eat of it your eyes will be opened, and you will be like God, knowing good and evil.'" The serpent's "craftiness" was the provision of assistance to a wrongdoer Eve with the intent to further an offense's commission. That is, the serpent aided and abetted Eve in stealing and eating the forbidden fruit (facilitation). The crime of facilitation "requires that a wrongful act be carried out."

The serpent acted to get Adam and Eve to break God's law. The guilt of the serpent was established with him agreeing with Satan and then working to get Eve to commit the criminal act of stealing the fruit.

Since the crimes against God's law in the garden started with the serpent, the serpent was judged first.

To the serpent, God said, "Because you have done this, you are cursed more than all cattle, and more than every beast of the field; on your belly you shall go, and you shall

---

[52] *United States v Hansen*, 599 U. S. ____ (2023), Slip, Op. at 6.
[53] Id.
[54] Id.
[55] 2 Corinthians 11:3.
[56] *United States v Hansen*, Slip, Op. at 7.

eat dust all the days of your life."[57] The greatest of the creatures in the field[58] who stood tall was cursed to slither on the floor among all creatures now standing above him. His wisdom was brought low.

Satan was guilty of criminal trespass, fraud, and solicitation/facilitation to commit theft by getting Eve to take the fruit. Satan was guilty of criminal trespass because he had no right to be in the garden, for he had been expelled from heaven and all of God's creation because of the rebellion he fostered among the angels of heaven. Satan also committed fraud by tricking Eve. As Jesus said of Satan, he is "the devil … He was a murderer from the beginning, and does not stand in the truth, because there is no truth in him. When he speaks a lie, he speaks from his own resources, for he is a liar and the father of it."[59]

Satan had entered the serpent so as to have physical entry into Eden. So while looking at the serpent, God was actually speaking to Satan,[60] and He said to him, "I will put enmity . . . between your seed and her Seed; He shall bruise your head, and you shall bruise His heel."[61]

God's sentence was that Satan, in time, would be captured and imprisoned[62] by the hand of the Son of Man,[63] whose robe proclaimed Him as King of Kings and Lord of Lords.[64] As Daniel[65] and John[66] reveal in their visions, under God's eternal plan, Satan will have his day of judgment, and his punishment will come. Under God's eternal plan to defeat

---

[57] Genesis 3:14.

[58] Genesis 3:1.

[59] John 8:44.

[60] See Revelation 12:9 ("So the great dragon was cast out, that serpent of old, called the Devil and Satan, who deceives the whole world; he was cast to the earth, and his angels were cast out with him."); Revelation 20:2; Revelation 12:15; 2 Corinthians 11:3.

[61] Genesis 3:15. See also Revelation 12:2–5.

[62] Revelation 19:20; 20:2.

[63] Daniel 7:13.

[64] Revelation 17:14.

[65] Daniel 7:26; 8:25.

[66] Revelation 19:19–20; 20:1–10.

the power and nature of evil before defeating Satan himself, Jesus came to earth as a man.

Jesus in human form defeated Satan on earth both in the desert[67] and after the cross. When He arose on the third day He said, "All power is given unto me in heaven and in earth."[68] His victory over Satan in the desert was recompense for the defeat of Adam by the words of Satan. His victory over Satan in death allowed Jesus to take the keys of sin and death[69] from Satan. In doing so, He made a mockery of him before all of heaven.[70]

In the final days, as Daniel and John explain, Satan will have power as a man on earth and will be defeated by Jesus and the armies of heaven and he will be cast into a fire forever. As Isaiah and Ezekiel both record, in the day of his final judgment, Satan will not escape the mocking of all creation.

Your pomp is brought down to Sheol, And the sound of your stringed instruments... "How you are fallen from heaven, O Lucifer, son of the morning! How you are cut down to the ground, You who weakened the nations!...Yet you shall be brought down to Sheol, To the lowest depths of the Pit. "Those who see you will gaze at you, And consider you, saying: 'Is this the man who made the earth tremble, Who shook kingdoms, Who made the world as a wilderness And destroyed its cities... '"[71]

"By the abundance of your trading You became filled with violence within, And you sinned;... Your

---

[67] Matthew 4:1–11; Luke 4:1–13.
[68] Matthew 28:18; Hebrews 2:14 ("that through death he might destroy him that had the power of death, that is, the devil").
[69] Revelation 1:18; Luke 10:17, 19 ("Then the seventy returned with joy, saying, 'Lord, even the demons are subject to us in Your name'...Behold, I give you the authority to trample ... over all the power of the enemy, and nothing shall by any means hurt you.").
[70] Colossians 2:15.
[71] Isaiah 14:11–12, 16–17.

*heart was lifted up because of your beauty; You
corrupted your wisdom for the sake of your splendor;... By the multitude of your iniquities, By the
iniquity of your trading;... I turned you to ashes
upon the earth In the sight of all who saw you. All
who knew you among the peoples are astonished at
you; You have become a horror, And shall be no
more forever."* [72]

God's judgment will be complete.

Turning to Eve, she was guilty of theft and criminal solici-
tation/felicitation to get Adam to break God's law. To Eve,
God said, "I will greatly multiply your sorrow . . . In pain,
you shall bring forth children . . . your husband . . . shall rule
over you."[73]

Turning to Adam, he was guilty of receiving stolen property, theft, and high treason. He was guilty of receiving stolen
property by taking the fruit from Eve, and theft by eating the
fruit.

He was guilty of high treason because he brought disobedience into the world—"Nevertheless death reigned from
Adam to Moses, even over those who had not sinned according to the likeness of the transgression of Adam."[74]

And by his actions, Adam sentenced all mankind to separation from a perfect relationship with God. "Through one
man's offense judgment came to all men, resulting in condemnation . . . by one man's disobedience, many were made
sinners."[75]

The treason was Adam's, not Eve's. "For Adam was first
formed; then Eve. And Adam was not seduced; but the
woman, being seduced, was in the transgression."[76]

Adam knew Satan was lying, but he followed his wife.
The high treason was amplified by the fact that because of

---

[72] Ezekiel 28:16–19.
[73] Genesis 3:16.
[74] Romans 5:14.
[75] Romans 5:18–19.
[76] 1 Timothy 2:13–14 (DRA).

Adam's sin, "Against its will, all creation was subjected to God's curse."[77]

When God issued the law not to eat the fruit of the Tree of the Knowledge of Good and Evil, God spoke to Adam not Eve. Thus when Adam ate of the tree, God said to Adam, not Eve, you "hast eaten of the tree, of which I commanded thee, saying, Thou shalt not eat of it"[78]

Under this conviction, God issued judgment. God said, "Because you have heeded the voice of your wife ... cursed is the ground . . . in toil you shall eat of it all the days of your life. Both thorns and thistles, it shall bring forth for you . . . In the sweat of your face, you shall eat bread."[79]

Further, eternal life in the physical body was taken away from Adam. God said, "Out of the ground . . . you were taken, for dust you are, and to dust you shall return."[80]

As a result of Adam's treason, all the earth is in disarray compared to its perfection before Adam's fall. God ruled that there would be a day the earth would be redeemed. The redemption was within God's ruling that Jesus would bruise the head of Satan and that Jesus would redeem all creation.

As Paul wrote, "all creation is waiting eagerly for that future day . . . when it will join God's children in glorious freedom from death and decay. For we know that all creation has been groaning as in the pains of childbirth right up to the present time."[81]

After the sentencing of the serpent, Adam, Eve, and Satan, a question remains. In making the law regarding the forbidden fruit, God said, "You shall surely die." But Adam and Eve, though punished, did not physically die. So what became of the law God issued?

First, the death with respect to Adam and Eve was the death of the perfect relationship they had with God in a perfect environment without the need to contend with evil. In

[77] Romans 8:20 (NLT).
[78] Genesis 3:17 (KJV).
[79] Genesis 3:17–19.
[80] Genesis 3:19.
[81] Romans 8:19, 21–22 (NLT).

this new state of existence, they were separated from God. They were no longer perfect in their relationship with Him. Now having an independent knowledge of good and evil, they now had to live with the consequences of both in operation on the earth.

Returning to the law God had imposed regarding the tree, there was, in fact, a physical death in compliance with the law as given. As Genesis records, "for Adam and his wife the Lord God made tunics of skin, and clothed them."[82] Where did the skin come from? It came from an animal. The law of blood sacrifice to atone for sin was instituted.[83] God sacrificed the animal and made clothes for Adam and Eve with its skin. The innocent blood of the animal atoned for their crimes and allowed God to make reconciliation. The atonement and reconciliation provided a just God with legal authority, the legal right, to protect Adam and Eve in their new state of imperfection and sin, which had caused separation from God.

After God judged and atoned for their sin through blood sacrifice, Adam and Eve were still in the garden and the Tree of Life was within their grasp. The fruit of that tree would make Adam and Eve immortal in their sin nature and unable to change. God looked upon Adam in his state of sin and rebellion and said, "And now, lest he put out his hand and

---

82 Genesis 3:21.

83 Hebrews 9:22 ("Without shedding of blood, there is no remission"); Leviticus 17:6 ("And the priest shall sprinkle the blood on the altar of the Lord at the door of the tabernacle of meeting, and burn the fat for a sweet aroma to the Lord"); Exodus 12:21–23 ("Pick out and take lambs for yourselves…and kill the Passover lamb…and strike the lintel and the two doorposts with the blood … [and] when He sees the blood… the Lord will pass over the door and not allow the destroyer to come into your houses to strike you"); Hebrews 9:1–7 ("The ark of the covenant…in which were the golden pot that had the manna, Aaron's rod that budded, and the tablets of the covenant; and above it were the cherubim of glory overshadowing the mercy seat. … The high priest…not without blood…offered for himself and for the people's sins.").

take also of the tree of life, and eat, and live forever—therefore the Lord God sent him out of the garden of Eden."[84]

God removed Adam and Eve from the garden not because of their disobedience, but because of their state of imperfection. If they became spiritually immortal by eating from the Tree of Life, their sin nature would remain without any ability for rectification with a perfect and sinless God. Thus, they had to leave Eden to protect them from eating from the Tree of Life.

His desire for reconciliation with Adam and Eve and their proceeding generations led God to remove them from Eden and place them instead into the wilderness to protect them from compounding their sin beyond reconciliation. Thus, the concept of incarceration—banishment, the removal of an offender from society—and placing the offender in a different location was introduced as a method of justice.

Two other concepts of justice made appearances. Justice, as discussed below, requires that the law be honored and enforced. Under God's law regarding the tree, God had a right to demand physical death from Adam and Eve. But God wanted mercy to prevail and He wanted to provide restoration. So God looked past punishment and found a way to apply both grace and mercy.

Mercy is not receiving the punishment that one deserves for actions taken; it is the suspension and withholding of earned consequences.

Grace is receiving what is not deserved or earned; it is undeserved favor.

The demand and requirement of the law—"you shall surely die"—was tempered by mercy and grace. God clothed Adam and Eve with the atoning blood of His sacrifice and protected them from committing a worse sin—eating from the Tree of Life. Through the blood sacrifice, His law remained enforced, but mercy prevailed. This process, accord-

---

[84] Genesis 3:22–23.

ing to the New Testament,[85] was made perfect and complete with Jesus on the cross and His resurrection.[86]

⚖️

The first criminal trial of mankind established the principle that justice involves the enforcement of the law and the application of punishment for disobedience. But the higher purposes of justice are mercy, grace, mitigation, reconciliation, and rehabilitation.[87] God-established justice is defined, in part, as restoration through changing of behavior. As God said through the prophet Ezekiel:

Again, when I say to the wicked, "You shall surely die," if he turns from his sin and does what is lawful and right, if the wicked restores the pledge, gives back what he has stolen, and walks in the statutes of life without committing iniquity, he shall surely live; he shall not die. None of his sins which he has committed shall be remembered against him; he has done what is lawful and right; he shall surely live.

---

[85] Ephesians 1:7; 1 John 1:7–9; 1 Peter 1:20.

[86] Colossians 1:13 ("He has delivered us from the power of darkness and [a]conveyed us into the kingdom of the Son of His love"); Colossians 2:13–15 ("And you, being dead in your trespasses and the uncircumcision of your flesh, He has made alive together with Him, having forgiven you all trespasses, having wiped out the handwriting of requirements that was against us, which was contrary to us. And He has taken it out of the way, having nailed it to the cross. Having disarmed principalities and powers, He made a public spectacle of them, triumphing over them in it."); Revelation 12:10–11 ("Then I heard a loud voice saying in heaven, 'Now salvation, and strength, and the kingdom of our God, and the power of His Christ have come, for the accuser of our brethren, who accused them before our God day and night, has been cast down. And they overcame him by the blood of the Lamb and by the word of their testimony, and they did not love their lives to the death.'").

[87] See 2 Corinthians 5.

Yet, the children of your people say, "The way of the Lord is not fair." But it is their way which is not fair! When the righteous turns from his righteousness and commits iniquity, he shall die because of it. But when the wicked turns from his wickedness and does what is lawful and right, he shall live because of it. Yet, you say, "The way of the Lord is not fair." O house of Israel, I will judge every one of you according to his own ways.[88]

In the trial of Adam and Eve and the sanctioning of all parties involved in the crime, the three daughters of justice—law, mercy, and grace—came into operation. The God of justice requires that the law be enforced and obeyed, but He tempers the harsh and unyielding application of the law through the sisters of the law—mercy and grace.

After their trial, time moved on, and Adam and Eve were fruitful and had children. The Bible tells the story of jealousy and murder involving two of their sons, resulting in the second criminal trial of man before the throne of God.

Abel was a keeper of sheep, and Cain was a tiller of the ground. In the process of time, it came to pass that Cain brought an offering of the fruit of the ground to the Lord. Abel also brought of the firstborn of his flock and of the fat thereof.[89] We are told that the Lord respected Abel and his offering, but He did not respect Cain and his offering. As a result, Cain was very angry, and his countenance fell.[90]

God rejected Cain's offering because it came from the ground, which God had cursed as a result of Adam's sin. The law of sacrifice was that God would accept the blood of a sacrificial lamb. Both Cain and Abel knew this. Cain's sin of

---

[88] Ezekiel 33:14–20.
[89] Genesis 4:2–4.
[90] Genesis 4:5.

disobedience to the law of sacrifice was compounded by his rage and pride.

It is recorded that God, in His justice, did not reject Cain. For God Himself spoke with Cain and said, "Why art thou wroth? And why is thy countenance fallen? If thou doest well, shalt thou not be accepted?"[91]

But what is more interesting is what God tells Cain after, encouraging him to do as he knows is right. God said, "If you do not do well, sin lies at the door."[92]

God warned Cain that the emotions of anger and rage, which were growing inside him, were sin. God warned Cain regarding his emotions: "Its desire is for you, but you should rule over it."[93]

God was warning him to get control of his emotions, or they would get control over him. God was concerned with what was going on in Cain's heart, as well as what he physically did.

Through this concern, Western legal tradition established the difference between *mens rea* ("evil mind, evil decision") and *actus reus* ("evil act"). Both must be present for a crime to occur.

God's justice warned Cain that he was considering evil, and such consideration always occurs before evil is done.

God established that justice is defined by what is in the heart of a man, not simply the behavior of a man. As He would later explain to His prophet, "The Lord does not see as man sees; for man looks at the outward appearance, but the Lord looks at the heart."[94]

Cain did not heed the warning from God, and when Cain spoke with his brother, his rage got the better of him, and he killed Abel.

After killing Abel Cain was put on trial and God said, "Where is Abel thy brother?" And at the second criminal

---

[91] Genesis 4:6–7 (KJV).
[92] Genesis 4:7.
[93] Genesis 4:7.
[94] 1 Samuel 16:7.

trial before the court of God, Cain said, "I know not: Am I my brother's keeper?"[95]

The court then heard from the only witness to the crime. "The voice of thy brother's blood crieth unto me from the ground."[96] With the evidence beyond a reasonable doubt that Cain had killed Abel established, God issued judgment and banished Cain from society and mankind—"a fugitive and a vagabond shalt thou be in the earth."[97] But Cain appealed to God for clemency and said,

> *My punishment is greater than I can bear! Surely,*
> *You have driven me out this day from the face of the*
> *ground; I shall be hidden from Your face; I shall be*
> *a fugitive and a vagabond on the earth, and it will*
> *happen that anyone who finds me will kill me.*[98]

God heard the appeal, considered it, and commuted his sentence:

> *And the Lord said to him, "Therefore, whoever kills*
> *Cain, vengeance shall be taken on him sevenfold."*
> *And the Lord set a mark on Cain, lest anyone find-*
> *ing him should kill him.*
>
> *Then Cain went out from the presence of the Lord*
> *and dwelt in the land of Nod, on the east of Eden.*
> *And Cain knew his wife, and she conceived and*
> *bore Enoch. And he built a city, and called the*
> *name of the city after the name of his son—Enoch.*[99]

God's justice seeks reconciliation and mercy. Cain surely deserved the full measure of punishment for murder, but God sought restoration, not death.

When Cain cried out that others would kill him, God put His protection on him and Cain was able to reintegrate into

---

95 Genesis 4:9 (KJV).
96 Genesis 4:10 (KJV).
97 Genesis 4:11–12 (KJV).
98 Genesis 4:13–14.
99 Genesis 4:15–17.

society. He went out from the Lord and built a city. In commuting Cain's sentence, God's justice established the concept of rehabilitation. God's justice seeks repentance over retribution because He wants reconciliation, and He seeks it through the application of mercy and grace.

From the days of Cain and Abel and the societies their children built, God defined what justice should be. The stories of the rise of the children of Abraham and the age of the Gentiles together established the meaning and application of justice between and among men.

B. Blessed is the man who executes justice for the oppressed, who gives food to the hungry; for the Lord also watches over the helpless and the defenseless[100]

In the movie *Law Abiding Citizen*, a father whose family was butchered, seeks revenge on the self-serving prosecutor who failed to keep his word and prosecute the killers of his family. The father killed the men who murdered his family, buried alive the defense attorney who orchestrated an unjust plea bargain for one of the murderers, and killed the judge who authorized the plea deal. After all this, the prosecutor asked him, "What principle was at work when you tortured and killed those people?"

The father answered, "Justice should be harsh, Nick, but especially for those who denied it to others [and] that everyone must be held accountable for their actions. In my experience, Nick, lessons not learned in blood are soon forgotten."[101]

---

[100] See Psalm 146:7–9. See also Psalm 106:3 ("Blessed are those who keep justice, and he who does righteousness at all times!").

[101] *Law Abiding Citizen*, directed by F. Gary Gray, written by Kurt Wimmer, featuring Jamie Foxx and Gerard Butler (West Hollywood, CA: The Film Department, 2009).

The Law of Moses would not find disagreement with this father's sentiment. Admittedly, there is harshness to the Law of Moses, but there is a context for the harshness, and even in its harshness, the primacy of the mercy and justice of God is still evident.

i. The Law of Moses: Purpose and Meaning

The Books of Exodus, Leviticus, Numbers, and Deuteronomy established the Law of Moses, which came into being during the time when the children of Abraham were freed from four hundred years of slavery in Egypt and had crossed into a land filled with various nations who had pagan religious traditions. When the children of Israel crossed over the Jordan, the Lord spoke to Moses.

> *Now the Lord spoke to Moses in the plains of Moab by the Jordan, across from Jericho, saying, "Speak to the children of Israel, and say to them: 'When you have crossed the Jordan into the land of Canaan, then you shall drive out all the inhabitants of the land from before you, destroy all their engraved stones, destroy all their molded images, and demolish all their high places; you shall dispossess the inhabitants of the land and dwell in it, for I have given you the land to possess. And you shall divide the land by lot as an inheritance among your families; to the larger you shall give a larger inheritance, and to the smaller you shall give a smaller inheritance; there everyone's inheritance shall be whatever falls to him by lot. You shall inherit according to the tribes of your fathers. But if you do not drive out the inhabitants of the land from before you, then it shall be that those whom you let remain shall be irritants in your eyes and thorns in your sides, and they shall harass you in the land where*

you dwell. Moreover, it shall be that I will do to you as I thought to do to them.'"[102]

No doubt this sounds harsh. But God had given the land to the Jews, and He wanted them to be safe in it.

> *When the Lord your God brings you into the land which you go to possess, and has cast out many nations before you, the Hittites and the Girgashites and the Amorites and the Canaanites and the Perizzites and the Hivites and the Jebusites, seven nations greater and mightier than you, and when the Lord your God delivers them over to you, you shall conquer them and utterly destroy them. You shall make no covenant with them . . . . For they will turn your sons away from following Me, to serve other gods; so the anger of the Lord will be aroused against you and destroy you suddenly. But thus you shall deal with them: you shall destroy their altars, and break down their sacred pillars, and cut down their wooden images, and burn their carved images with fire.[103]*

He told them that the land was theirs. They were to make it safe for themselves and remove those things that would otherwise harass them. The story of the Jews in the promised land is that for generations they continuously failed to follow God's advice and laws.

Justice sometimes can be harsh when it seeks to cleanse and remove corrupting influences. God told them before they crossed the Jordan that He wanted the inhabitants of the land removed because "they will turn your sons away from following Me." They were His children, and He wanted to prevent the possibility of their corruption.

The theories of justice include incapacitation, preventing an evil from reoccurring, and incarceration (banishment).

---

[102] Numbers 33:50–56.
[103] Deuteronomy 7:1–2, 4–5.

God's justice required both regarding the evil of those who inhabited the land, so the land would be safe for His people.

It was God's plan to make room for the Jews and to bless them[104] in the new land and they were His chosen people. Then God made clear that not only were they His chosen people, but that status means something regarding how they were to behave in the face of all that existed on the earth. They were to be a separate people.

> *For you are a holy people to the Lord your God; the Lord your God has chosen you to be a people for Himself, a special treasure above all the peoples on the face of the earth. The Lord did not set His love on you nor choose you because you were more in number than any other people, for you were the least of all peoples; but because the Lord loves you, and because He would keep the oath which He swore to your fathers, the Lord has brought you out with a mighty hand, and redeemed you from the house of bondage, from the hand of Pharaoh king of Egypt.*[105]

> *I will send My fear before you...which shall drive out the Hivite, the Canaanite, and the Hittite from before you. .... Little by little I will drive them out from before you, until you have increased, and you inherit the land. ... You shall make no covenant with them, nor with their gods. They shall not dwell in your land, lest they make you sin against Me. For if you serve their gods, it will surely be a snare to you.*[106]

---

[104] Exodus 23:25–26 ("So you shall serve the Lord your God, and He will bless your bread and your water. And I will take sickness away from the midst of you. No one shall suffer miscarriage or be barren in your land; I will fulfill the number of your days.").

[105] Deuteronomy 7:6–8. See also Deuteronomy 26:18–19.

[106] Exodus 23:27–33.

But the problem was that the Jews, though following God, also served other gods and proved to be stubborn in following the word of God.[107] Moses himself records that while speaking with God, the Lord said to Moses, "'I have seen this people, and indeed it is a stiff-necked people!'"[108]

The harshness of God's laws that He imposed on the Jews was born out of the need to keep them in line under His leadership because they were a rebellious people.[109] The harshness of the Law was also to establish a clear understanding between right and wrong.[110] The Law came to remove four hundred years of Egypt from their minds and value systems.

Justice includes the concept of discipline and obedience, as they are required by the Law. It was because of their behavior that God led them into the promised land with a hard hand.[111] As God Himself said to Moses regarding His nature,

> *The Lord, the Lord God, merciful and gracious, long-suffering, and abounding in goodness and truth, keeping mercy for thousands, forgiving iniquity and transgression and sin, by no means clearing the guilty, visiting the iniquity of the fathers upon the children and the children's children to the third and the fourth generation.*[112]

> *Therefore know that the Lord your God, He is God, the faithful God who keeps covenant and mercy for a thousand generations with those who love Him and keep His commandments; and He repays those who hate Him to their face, to destroy them.*

---

[107] Deuteronomy 10:16; see also Isaiah 43:22–24; Malachi 3:8–9; Joshua 24:2, 6, 14.

[108] Exodus 32:9.

[109] Exodus 33:3, 5; Deuteronomy 31:16, 19, 21; Deuteronomy 31:22, 24–29; Ezekiel 2:3–4.

[110] See Leviticus 18–20 for an example of God defining right from wrong.

[111] Exodus 23:20–24.

[112] Exodus 34:6–7.

He will not be slack with him who hates Him; He will repay him to his face. Therefore you shall keep the commandments, the statutes, and the judgments which I command you today, to observe them.[113]

I will be gracious to whom I will be gracious, and I will have compassion on whom I will have compassion.[114]

Justice is complicated. It remembers all sin yet it shows mercy. Justice promises that those who do evil are to be punished, but justice determines when and how punishments will be applied and if mercy and grace will prevail over the demands of punishment under law.

The Law of Moses reflects the complicated nature of justice and how it functioned with a stiff-necked, rebellious, and hardhearted people. Matthew records how Jesus explained the origin of the Law of Moses:

The Pharisees also came to Him, testing Him, and saying to Him, "Is it lawful for a man to divorce his wife for just any reason?"

And He answered and said to them, "Have you not read . . . 'For this reason, a man shall leave his father and mother and be joined to his wife, and the two shall become one flesh'? So then, they are no longer two but one flesh. Therefore what God has joined together, let not man separate."

They said to Him, "Why then did Moses command to give a certificate of divorce, and to put her away?"

He said to them, "Moses, because of the hardness of your hearts, permitted you to divorce your wives . . . ."[115]

---

[113] Deuteronomy 7:9–11.
[114] Exodus 33:19.
[115] Matthew 19:3–8.

The Law of Moses evolved for two reasons: first, to separate the behavior of the Jews from the other peoples of the promised land, and second, to prove to them that they were not holy by their own action, and they needed God to be holy.[116]

The harshness and absoluteness of the Law was designed to define holiness and to be a mirror to behavior, the result being the conclusion that mankind could not be holy on its own. "Whoever shall keep the whole law, and yet stumble in one point, he is guilty of all."[117] The purpose of the Law was to convince mankind it needs a savior from the sin in his nature and the inability to be perfect in the face of God in both mind and action. As Paul explains,

> *Now we know that whatever the law says, it says to those who are under the law, that every mouth may be stopped, and all the world may become guilty before God. Therefore by the deeds of the law no flesh will be justified in His sight, for by the law is the knowledge of sin.[118]*

> *What purpose then does the law serve? It was added because of transgressions, till the Seed should come to whom the promise was made; and it was appointed through angels by the hand of a mediator. Now, a mediator does not mediate for one only, but God is one.*

> *Is the law then against the promises of God? Certainly not! For if there had been a law given which could have given life, truly righteousness would have been by the law. But the Scripture has confined all under sin, that the promise by faith in Jesus Christ might be given to those who believe. But before faith came, we were kept under guard by the*

---

[116] Romans 3:9, 19–20, 23–24; Romans 8:1–8.
[117] James 2:10.
[118] Romans 3:19–22.

law, kept for the faith which would afterward be revealed.

Therefore the law was our tutor to bring us to Christ, that we might be justified by faith. But after faith has come, we are no longer under a tutor.[119]

The purpose of law is to define evil, and through the law, justice can be applied when appealed to through a mediator. Grace and mercy allow for a bridge between the law and justice. There is a distinction that separates the power of the law from justice. The nature of the law, as compared to justice, is that the law is only concerned with obedience, order, and what is required. The law seeks to define, not to nurture.

To be sure, many of the laws Moses imposed were indeed without pity and would today seem backward and cruel. Moses did command that a virgin who is raped but is not betrothed to another man does not have her honor justified by the death of her rapist; she was rather required to marry her rapist, and he would lose the right to divorce her.[120] However, a virgin who is betrothed does enjoy the justice of the death of her attacker.[121]

Moses also decreed that rebellious children were to be stoned if the parents declared they were incorrigible,[122] and that if a wife aids her husband when he is attacked by another male and touches the genitals of the attacking male, "then you shall cut off her hand; your eye shall not pity her."[123]

The harshness of the Law provides background for the truth that the nature of the law without its sisters, grace and mercy, is cold and without pity in its application. The Law of Moses included fifty-four verses in one chapter alone that were dedicated to the curses God would bring upon Israel for failure to obey the Law. The list of curses included everything from financial failure to suffering all types of plagues,

---

[119] Galatians 3:19–25.
[120] Deuteronomy 22:28–29.
[121] Deuteronomy 22:25.
[122] Deuteronomy 21:18–21.
[123] Deuteronomy 25:11–12.

to being militarily conquered, to being sent back to Egypt for slavery.[124]

ii. The Law of Moses: The Heart of God

A closer reading of the Law of Moses and the commands of God reflects a deeper purpose for the Law and of God's heart. The Law of Moses was designed to bring the children of Abraham, and all mankind, to know the heart of God— mercy and grace. David would write upon reflection on the laws of God, "Deal bountifully with Your servant, that I may live and keep Your word. Open my eyes, that I may see wondrous things from Your law."[125]

In reflecting on the Law, David concluded (1) that God's law is just and right; (2) that God honors appeals to His law and sees obedience to it; (3) that obedience to His law brings happiness; (4) that knowing His Word brings wisdom and peace in the face of those who do evil; and (5) under the Law, God's protection can be sought from those who do evil.[126]

The Law of Moses was a reflection of justice by the outcome of obedience. Because of its limited purpose, the Law of Moses was not the full expression of God's justice—mercy and grace. Seeing God's grace and mercy within the operation of the Law of Moses is what separates and distinguishes David as "a man after [God's] own heart"[127] and allowed him to write the Psalms.

The Law of Moses was not God's best illumination of His justice; it was a start in defining right and wrong and establishing that justice exists under the eyes of God.[128]

---

[124] Deuteronomy 28:15–68.

[125] Psalm 119:17–18.

[126] Psalm 119.

[127] 1 Samuel 13:14; Acts 13:22 ("He raised up for them David as king, to whom also He gave testimony and said, 'I have found David the son of Jesse, a man after My own heart, who will do all My will.'").

[128] Romans 3:19–20.

There is a difference between the law and its sisters, mercy and grace. The law is strict in judgment and condemnation; its sisters—mercy and grace—say, "Neither do I condemn you; go and sin no more."[129]

God's mercy and grace, in the mouth of one wronged, says, "Lord, do not charge them with this sin."[130] It says, "Father, forgive them; for they know not what they do."[131] "Mercy triumphs over judgment."[132]

Consider the stories of the great cities Sodom, Gomorrah, and Nineveh, which illustrate the difference between punishment—that is, retribution—and mercy—that is, rehabilitation or restoration.

We are told that in the story of Sodom and Gomorrah, if ten righteous men were found in the city, God would have relented and saved the entire city for the sake of the ten. Sodom and Gomorrah was destroyed not because of sin, but because ten righteous men could not be found there. In the story of Nineveh, we are told they were a sinful city, but when offered repentance they took it, and God relented from His judgment that the city was to be destroyed.

Nineveh—modern-day Mosul, Iraq—was the capital of the Assyrian empire under King Sennacherib.[133] God sent Jonah to preach to Nineveh to get them to repent.[134] Jonah refused and famously ended up in the belly of a fish for three days and after he repented he went to Nineveh to do as God had commanded him.[135]

Under the words of Jonah and the behavior of the entire city, "God saw their works, that they turned from their evil way; and God relented from the disaster that He had said He would bring upon them, and He did not do it."[136]

---

[129] John 8:11.
[130] Acts 7:60.
[131] Luke 23:34.
[132] James 2:13.
[133] 2 Kings 19:36.
[134] Jonah 1:1–2.
[135] Jonah 3:5–9.
[136] Jonah 3:10.

But Jonah was angry that God gave Nineveh a chance to repent, and God answered, "Should I not pity Nineveh, that great city, in which are more than one hundred and twenty thousand persons who cannot discern between their right hand and their left—and much livestock?"[137]

The nature of justice, under God's eye and hand, is rehabilitation, rectification, and repentance in the face of disobedience to the Law. The purpose of law differs from justice in that the nature of the law is not concerned with the harshness of its operation; it is only concerned with obedience and the enforcement of sanctions for failing to obey. As the Old and New Testaments demonstrate, the distinction between law and justice is that the former is narrow in purpose, while the latter is broad in the outcome of its implementation and purpose.

iii. The Law of Moses: God Seeks Justice Not Obedience

As the children of Israel moved from a migrant people to a nation and a kingdom, the relationship between God and them adjusted. Justice soon became defined in terms of mercy and grace, not pure obedience to a rigid set of laws written on stones.[138] In the days of Jeremiah, it was written,

> *Behold, the days are coming, says the Lord, when I will make a new covenant with the house of Israel and with the house of Judah—not according to the covenant that I made with their fathers in the day that I took them by the hand to lead them out of the land of Egypt, My covenant which they broke . . . . But this is the covenant that I will make with the house of Israel . . . I will put My law in their minds, and write it on their hearts; and I will*

---

[137] Jonah 4:11.
[138] Deuteronomy 27: 3, 8–9 (NKJV); Deuteronomy 30:19; 31:26; Joshua 24:27.

> *be their God, and they shall be My people. . . . For I*
> *will forgive their iniquity, and their sin I will re-*
> *member no more.*[139]

During the seventy-year captivity of Judah in Babylon, God made a promise to the children of Israel:

> *I will give you a new heart and put a new spirit*
> *within you; I will take the heart of stone out of your*
> *flesh and give you a heart of flesh. I will put My*
> *Spirit within you and cause you to walk in My*
> *statutes, and you will keep My judgments and do*
> *them. Then you shall dwell in the land that I gave to*
> *your fathers; you shall be My people, and I will be*
> *your God.*[140]

Here God made clear that justice, in His eyes, was more than physical obedience; it was a heart that seeks to do justice, love mercy, and walk with Him.

But the creation of a new covenant begs the question: why make a new law and covenant in the first place? The purpose of the first covenant was achieved by creating order and by creating a people who were known as God's chosen people. If this was achieved through the Law of Moses, why promise a new covenant? Why promise to write it on their hearts and not on stone?

The answer is in the nature of God's justice and His desire for justice to reign over the requirements of the Law in the relationship between God and mankind. The new covenant enhanced the meaning of justice. The nature of the Law of Moses was that it was based on reciprocity. Under the Law of Moses, the relationship between man and God was *do this and I will do that*. But God wanted a warm relationship with man, so under the new covenant, God replaces man's heart of stone with a heart of flesh.

The Law of Moses without mercy and grace is harsh and can be cruel when applied. The nature of the Law required a

---

[139] Jeremiah 31:31–34.

[140] Ezekiel 36:26–28. See also Isaiah 59:21; Hebrews 10:16; 8:10.

new covenant. The Law, by its nature, is constraining and only requires obedience; justice, by its nature, is liberating and requires more than outward obedience.

2.

For the Lord Is a God of Justice,[1] and His Mercy Is Long-Suffering Forever[2]

Mercy triumphs over judgment.[3] The Bible establishes that justice is defined by what is done and why it is done. Justice is defined by doing right, being right, and seeking righteousness. Justice through law defines evil, but justice through grace and mercy provides a way for rectification and rehabilitation to prevail over judgment and punishment. The principle upholding the meaning of justice is that God's heart is just and fair.

A. Justice is defined by the heart of God[4]

As David wrote of the heart of God, exemplifying His justice, "The Lord opens the eyes of the blind; the Lord raises those who are bowed down; the Lord loves the righteous. The Lord watches over the strangers; He relieves the father-

---

[1] Isaiah 30:18.
[2] Exodus 34:6-7.
[3] Romans 7:4–6; James 2:12–13.
[4] Psalm 103:6–18; Proverbs 22:22–23; Matthew 11:2–6; Luke 1:51–55; Amos 5:14–15; Exodus 22:20–24; Psalm 41:1–3; Psalm 72:1–19; Zechariah 7:9–10; Psalm 9:9–15; Proverbs 21:13; Psalm 34:16–17 ("The face of the Lord is against those who do evil, To cut off the remembrance of them from the earth. The righteous cry out, and the Lord hears, And delivers them out of all their troubles.").

less and widow; but the way of the wicked He turns upside down."[5]

David also observed that the strength of a nation comes from understanding and implementing justice. "The King's strength also loves justice; You have established equity; You have executed justice and righteousness in Jacob."[6]

In defining the heart of God, David wrote, "For great is Your mercy toward me, And You have delivered my soul from the depths of Sheol.... You, O Lord, are a God full of compassion and gracious, long-suffering and abundant in mercy and truth."[7]

David wrote that justice in the hand of God is defined by fair adjudication between the guilty and the innocent, and fair determination regarding the aggrieved party in a dispute. David called upon the Lord to judge between himself and Saul and rule accordingly:

> *Look, this day your eyes have seen that the Lord delivered you today into my hand . . . But my eye spared you, and I said, "I will not stretch out my hand against my lord . . ." [S]ee the corner of your robe in my hand! . . . I have not sinned against you. Yet, you hunt my life to take it. Let the Lord judge between you and me, and let the Lord avenge me on you. . . . Therefore, let the Lord be judge, and judge between you and me, and see and plead my case, and deliver me out of your hand.*[8]

Because God had judged Saul fairly and saved David from an unjust king, David proclaimed, "You, Lord, have helped me and comforted me."[9] Justice defines how those with

---

[5] Psalm 146:8–9.

[6] Psalm 99:4.

[7] Psalm 86:13,15; see also Psalm 96:13 ("For He is coming, for He is coming to judge the earth. He shall judge the world with righteousness, and the peoples with His truth.").

[8] 1 Samuel 24:10–12, 15.

[9] Psalm 86:17.

power should rule, as illustrated by how God in heaven rules.

In the times of the prophets and kings of ancient Israel, the Scriptures make clear what God required of them. Centuries later in ceremonies to coronate the kings of England, when they received the sword to rule, a prayer was said over them. In the name of Christ Jesus, it was prayed that the king would

> ...not bear the sword in vain, but may use it as the Minister of God to resist evil and defend the good through Jesus Christ our Lord. Amen. Receive this kingly sword, may it be to you and to all who witness these things a sign and symbol, not of judgment, but of justice, not of might, but of mercy.[10]

This prayer and admonishment reflects the Western legal tradition that those who govern do so under the eye and judgment of God. The justice of God includes the concepts of the rule of law, equal and impartial application of the law, and the prevention of oppression of the poor, the weak, and the stranger—"Seek justice, Rebuke the oppressor; Defend the fatherless, Plead for the widow."[11]

When the kings of Judah and Israel did evil, God was angered by injustice, and He defined what the injustice was.

> How long will you judge unjustly, and show partiality to the wicked? Defend the poor and fatherless; do justice to the afflicted and needy; deliver the poor and needy; free them from the hand of the wicked.[12]

God defined injustice as the lack of impartial application of the Law and denying the protection of the Law to the weak because they were weak or subverting the fair application of the Law to benefit the strong because they were strong.

---

[10] Invocation by the Archbishop of Westminster, Coronation of King Charles III on May 6, 2023, Westminster Abbey, London England.

[11] Isaiah 1:17.

[12] Psalm 82:1–4.

> *Do not rob the poor because he is poor, nor oppress
> the afflicted at the gate; for the Lord will plead
> their cause, and plunder the soul of those who
> plunder them.*[13]

> *The king who judges the poor with truth, his
> throne will be established forever.*[14]

> *It is not for kings . . . to drink wine, nor for
> princes intoxicating drink; lest they drink and for-
> get the law, and pervert the justice of all the afflict-
> ed. . . . Open your mouth for the speechless, in the
> cause of all who are appointed to die. Open your
> mouth, judge righteously, and plead the cause of the
> poor and needy.*[15]

> *You shall do no injustice in judgment. You shall
> not be partial to the poor, nor honor the person of
> the mighty. In righteousness you shall judge your
> neighbor.*[16]

God made clear that what He demanded from the kings of
His people is what was done from His throne. "He will judge
Your people with righteousness . . . He will bring justice to
the poor of the people; He will save the children of the
needy, and will break in pieces the oppressor."[17]

Justice is defined by God—"For I, the Lord, love justice; I
hate robbery"[18]—and justice includes the control of governmental power and fair application of the law, as well as the
fact that God sees and judges the acts of those who govern—
"He is not partial to princes, nor does He regard the rich
more than the poor."[19] Justice also includes not being blind
to those without power.

---

[13] Proverbs 22:22–23.
[14] Proverbs 29:14.
[15] Proverbs 31:4–5, 8–9.
[16] Leviticus 19:15.
[17] Psalm 72:2–4.
[18] Isaiah 61:8.
[19] Job 34:19.

As David observed, God is "a father of the fatherless, a defender of widows . . . God sets the solitary in families; He brings out those who are bound into prosperity; but the rebellious dwell in a dry land."[20] For "He administers justice for the fatherless and the widow, and loves the stranger, giving him food and clothing."[21] And God commanded the children of Israel through Moses,

> *You shall neither mistreat a stranger nor oppress him, for you were strangers in the land of Egypt.*
>
> *You shall not afflict any widow or fatherless child. If you afflict them in any way, and they cry at all to Me, I will surely hear their cry; and My wrath will become hot, and I will kill you with the sword; your wives shall be widows, and your children fatherless.*[22]

God does not suffer the evil of kings, and they will have their day of judgment before the eye of God's judgment. God is not blind to injustice done. "Thus says the Lord of hosts: 'I will punish Amalek for what he did to Israel, how he ambushed him on the way when he came up from Egypt.'"[23]

But when God ordered just punishment, He also ruled that the innocent shall not suffer with the guilty. Abraham knew this of God, and he said to God, would you punish the innocent with the guilty?[24] It is recorded that under God's judgment on the Amalekites God's people said, "to the Kenites, 'Go, depart, get down from among the Amalekites, lest I destroy you with them. For you showed kindness to all the children of Israel when they came up out of Egypt.' So the Kenites departed from among the Amalekites."[25]

---

[20] Psalm 68:5–6.
[21] Deuteronomy 10:18.
[22] Exodus 22:21–24.
[23] 1 Samuel 15:2.
[24] Genesis 18:22–25.
[25] 1 Samuel 15:6.

Under God's justice two kings were judged for their actions. Due to the disobedience of King Saul, "Samuel said to Saul, 'I will not return with you, for you have rejected the word of the Lord, and the Lord has rejected you from being king over Israel.'"[26]

As to King Agag, when he was brought before the prophet Samuel, God's judgment on his evil was pronounced. The prophet said, "As your sword has made women childless, so shall your mother be childless among women."[27] After which, "Samuel hacked Agag in pieces before the Lord."[28]

Righteous indignation over injustice is reflected in the nature of justice, not the law. Justice, not the law, commands that the weak shall not be oppressed, and justice, not the law, requires both the protection and avenging of the powerless.

But justice also finds a way to forgive.

When Jesus was confronted with both a prostitute who through her tears begged for forgiveness at His feet as well as the arrogance of those with power who mocked her, Jesus said:

> *Do you see this woman? I came into your house*
> *[but you failed to extend to Me the usual courtesies*
> *shown to a guest]; you gave Me no water for My*
> *feet, but she has wet My feet with her tears and*
> *wiped them with her hair [demonstrating her love].*
> *You gave Me no [welcoming] kiss, but from the*
> *moment I came in, she has not ceased to kiss My*
> *feet. You did not [even] anoint My head with [ordi-*
> *nary] oil, but she has anointed My feet with [costly*
> *and rare] perfume. Therefore I say to you, her sins,*
> *which are many, are forgiven . . . Then He said to*
> *her, "Your sins are forgiven." Those who were re-*
> *clining at the table with Him began saying among*
> *themselves, "Who is this who even forgives sins?"*
> *Jesus said to the woman, "Your faith [in Me] has*

---

[26] 1 Samuel 15:26.
[27] 1 Samuel 15:33.
[28] 1 Samuel 15:33.

*saved you; go in peace [free from the distress expe-
rienced because of sin]."*[29]

Jesus listed the social insults and the sin of those with power
who did not greet Him properly. He did this in order to honor
the woman of sin who did honor Him in their midst. In so
doing, Jesus displayed and elevated the purpose of justice
over the Law. Although the Pharisees were right that under
the Law, it was forbidden for the unclean—the prostitute—to
be touched by the clean—Jesus, a rabbi. But Jesus, being
just, was more concerned with the weightier issues of justice: forgiveness, righteousness, and reconciliation.[30]

Justice involves doing what makes the law worthy to be
supported and obeyed.

Consider how Jesus dealt with the Law that forbade work
on the Sabbath. Jesus was in the synagogue, and a man with
a withered hand was there, and the self-serving priests asked
Him—so they could accuse Him of breaking the Law—
whether it was lawful to heal on the Sabbath. Jesus answered
by asking how many of the priests would rescue their sheep
from a ditch on the Sabbath. Therefore, Jesus argued, it is
lawful to do good on the Sabbath, and He healed the man.
On that day, the priests became determined to kill Jesus.[31]

The point of the Law prohibiting work on the Sabbath was
that God had established the Sabbath and made it holy. A day
that is holy does not prohibit doing good; it prohibits doing
work for one's own selfish benefit.

Justice focuses on the weightier issues of the law. The law,
unlike justice, is brutal in execution because it is written in
stone and is designed not to allow for nuances in application.

The law is designed to establish order and regulation without distinction. But justice seeks to make the broken whole
and to protect the helpless. This is the meaning behind
Matthew quoting Isaiah: "A bruised reed He will not break,

---

[29] Luke 7:44–50 (AMP).
[30] Matthew 23:23.
[31] Matthew 12:9–14. See also Luke 3:10–17 for the story of Jesus healing the woman with the spirit of infirmity.

and smoking flax He will not quench."[32] Justice, in the hand of Jesus, does not break the bruised nor quench small starts, but the Law, in the hand of the priests, will show no mercy if that is what is required on its face.

The law, by its nature, is only concerned with what it requires and its demand for obedience regardless of the outcome. Justice, by its nature, is more demanding and does not confuse obedience with honoring the purpose of the Law. As the Prophet Micah famously said:

> *With what shall I come before the Lord, And bow myself before the High God? Shall I come before Him with burnt offerings, With calves a year old?*
>
> *Will the Lord be pleased with thousands of rams,*
>
> *Ten thousand rivers of oil? Shall I give my firstborn for my transgression, The fruit of my body for the sin of my soul?*
>
> *He has shown you, O man, what is good; And what does the Lord require of you But to do justly, To love mercy, And to walk humbly with your God?*[33]

The nature of the operation of the law, unlike justice, has no capacity to rectify or to rescue a person from the requirements of the law or the judgment for failing to comply with those requirements. Nor does the nature of the operation of the law require mercy. The law provides order, not justice.

The law is what is required by society; justice is what is desired by society. The law requires obedience; it does not provide or promise mercy. The law is about the correctness of output and outcome; justice includes equity of output and outcome. The point is that it is written that God is a God of Justice,[34] righteousness, and mercy[35] not a god of the law. God issued the Law only to maintain order.

---

[32] Matthew 12:20 (citing Isaiah 42:3).

[33] Micah 6:6–8.

[34] Isaiah 30:18.

[35] Deuteronomy 32:4; Psalm 89:14; Matthew 22:37–40.

Consider the difference between the law and justice, as seen in the execution of Jesus. When Jesus and the two thieves hung on the cross, the Pharisees asked Pontius Pilate to break the legs of the two men condemned with Jesus. The reason for this request was that the Law of Moses required the dead to be buried before the beginning of Passover.

Consider the voice of law without its sisters mercy and grace. The Pharisees, adhering to the Law of Moses, said break the legs of the suffering, so they can die faster to please us because the Law of Moses requires it.[36]

Consider another example of the merciless application of the Law and the absurdity of the Law without considering its purpose or the justice behind it. In John 9 we are told that on the Sabbath, Jesus healed a man who had been blind from birth. Under the Law, it was written that work was prohibited on the Sabbath, so the Pharisees condemned the healed man for carrying his bed and walking home on the Sabbath after he was healed by Jesus.

Rather than welcoming the man into the synagogue to celebrate his healing—when the man had said Jesus must be a prophet for what he had done—the Pharisees expelled him from the synagogue. The application of law, without context and justice, can produce ridiculous and harmful results because it is written in stone. That is why God said He would write a new law on a newly given heart of flesh—the new heart being something alive.

In defense of the Law of Moses, it was not without commands that justice be done. God defined justice by His own nature: "the Lord your God . . . shows no partiality nor takes a bribe. . . . Therefore love the stranger, for you were strangers in the land of Egypt."[37] "Now therefore, let the fear of the Lord be upon you; take care and do it, for there is no

---

[36] John 19:31.
[37] Deuteronomy 10:17–19.

iniquity with the Lord our God, no partiality, nor taking of bribes."[38] The Law of Moses included the requirement of seeing the pain and need of others. God commanded that the needs of the poor were not to be disregarded by His people. The Lord commanded:

> *If there is among you a poor man of your brethren, within any of the gates in your land which the Lord your God is giving you, you shall not harden your heart nor shut your hand from your poor brother, but you shall open your hand wide to him and willingly lend him sufficient for his need, whatever he needs. Beware lest there be a wicked thought in your heart, saying, "The seventh year, the year of release, is at hand," and your eye be evil against your poor brother, and you give him nothing, and he cry out to the Lord against you, and it becomes sin among you. You shall surely give to him, and your heart should not be grieved when you give to him because for this thing the Lord your God will bless you in all your works and in all to which you put your hand. For the poor will never cease from the land; therefore I command you, saying, "You shall open your hand wide to your brother, to your poor and your needy, in your land."*[39]

When God commanded that "You shall open your hand . . . to your poor and your needy," that included having compassion and pity, not condemnation.

God requires mercy and pity from His children to those in need, but He prohibits condescension in giving. As Herman Melville famously observed, "Of all the preposterous assumptions of humanity over humanity, nothing exceeds most

---

[38] 2 Chronicles 19:7.
[39] Deuteronomy 15:7–11.

of the criticisms made on the habits of the poor by the well-housed, well-warmed, and well-fed."[40]

Compassion for the poor and the weak by those who are blessed is required, but God requires that "your heart should not be grieved when you give to him." In God's view, justice is defined by what is done for the weak and poor and needy in the face of wealth and power.

Under the Law of Moses, written on stone as it was, God still made clear it was the heart of man that He was concerned with. As Jesus said, "Take heed that you do not do your charitable deeds before men, to be seen by them. Otherwise, you have no reward from your Father in heaven."[41]

"Every way of a man is right in his own eyes, But the Lord weighs the hearts."[42] Reflecting on the motivation of the heart and the actions of men, Jesus warned, do not do right to be seen by men so as to enjoy their accolades because that will be the only reward that you receive from heaven. But when you do right, not to be seen, but because it is right, God will see what you did in private and will reward you in the eyes of men.[43]

As Paul explained, when those who do right do so with the right heart, on the day of judgment before Jesus, the works will be honored and rewarded in heaven, but works done with the wrong heart will be burned up in the fire of the judgment of acts and motives.[44] Under the justice of God, motive, not just actions, matters.

---

[40] Herman Melville, "Poor Man's Pudding and Rich Man's Crumbs" in *Herman Melville: Pierre, Israel Potter, The Piazza Tales, The Confidence-Man, Billy Budd, and Uncollected Prose* (LOA, 1985) at 1234.

[41] Matthew 6:1.

[42] Proverbs 21:2.

[43] Matthew 6:2-4.

[44] 1 Corinthians 13:8–15.

Justice includes defending the weak and those without protection. "Lord, who is like You," David asked, "delivering the poor from him who is too strong for him?"[45]

King Solomon, under the Law of Moses, said, "He who sows iniquity will reap sorrow, and the rod of his anger will fail."

God made clear, "Do not rob the poor because he is poor, nor oppress the afflicted at the gate; for the Lord will plead their cause, and plunder the soul of those who plunder them."[46]

Justice is not a concept without defined behavior. God requires justice over sacrifice[47] and God makes clear, "Whoever shuts his ears to the cry of the poor will also cry himself and not be heard,"[48] but "He who follows righteousness and mercy finds life, righteousness, and honor."[49]

Justice in the eyes of God favors those who do justice for others. Not only, as David observed, "Happy is he...Who executes justice for the oppressed"[50] and it is "a joy for the just to do justice,"[51] but it is a gift from God to know what justice is, for those who do evil have no understanding of justice.[52]

Justice is not blind to evil, for it warns, "Woe to him who builds his house by unrighteousness and his chambers by

---

[45] Psalm 35:10; see also Psalm 34:17; Psalm 34:6 ("This poor man cried out and the Lord heard him and saved him out of all his troubles.").

[46] Proverbs 22:8, 22–23.

[47] Proverbs 21:3 ("To do righteousness and justice is more acceptable to the Lord than sacrifice.").

[48] Proverbs 21:13.

[49] Proverbs 21:21.

[50] Psalm 146:5,7. See also Psalm 72:1–4.

[51] Proverbs 21:15 ("But destruction will come to the workers of iniquity.").

[52] Proverbs 28:5 ("Evil men do not understand Justice, but those who seek the Lord understand all.").

injustice, who uses his neighbor's service without wages and gives him nothing for his work."[53]

The Bible defines what a just and righteous man is by how he lives:

> *He who walks uprightly, and works righteousness, and speaks the truth in his heart; he who does not backbite with his tongue, nor does evil to his neighbor, nor does he take up a reproach against his friend; in whose eyes a vile person is despised, but he honors those who fear the Lord; he who swears to his own hurt and does not change; he who does not put out his money at usury, nor does he take a bribe against the innocent. He who does these things shall never be moved.*[54]

Put another way, justice is what justice does. "To do justice to the fatherless and the oppressed, that the man of the earth may oppress no more."[55]

God's justice promises, "The needy shall not always be forgotten; the expectation of the poor shall not perish forever."[56]

Justice is defined by protecting the weak, remembering and considering the plight of those who are without help or defense, and preventing those with power and influence from taking advantage of their positions to the detriment of others. Justice includes helping the poor, for "he who has pity on the

---

[53] Jeremiah 22:13. See also Leviticus 19:13 ("'You shall not cheat your neighbor, nor rob him. The wages of him who is hired shall not remain with you all night until morning.").

[54] Psalm 15:2–5.

[55] Psalm 10:18; see also Proverbs 29:7 ("The righteous considers the cause of the poor, but the wicked does not understand such knowledge.").

[56] Psalm 9:18; Psalm 9:9–10, 12.

poor lends to the Lord, and he will pay back what he has given."⁵⁷

Justice takes up the defense of the defenseless under unjust punishment. As God gave Balaam's donkey the ability to speak up for herself and He sent the Angel of the Lord to speak up for her against Balaam's unjust beating of her,⁵⁸ God's justice also includes defending the weak and remembering what is done in His name.

But because justice also allows for time for the oppressor to repent, God can be accused of having a blind eye to injustice. When God was accused of turning a blind eye to those who obey Him while allowing those who do evil to prosper, God answered both concerns. The following conversation is recorded:

> *"Your words have been harsh against Me," says the Lord, "Yet you say, 'What have we spoken against You?' You have said, 'It is useless to serve God; What profit is it that we have kept His ordinance, and that we have walked as mourners before the Lord of hosts? So now we call the proud blessed, for those who do wickedness are raised up; they even tempt God and go free.'"*

> *Then those who feared the Lord spoke to one another, and the Lord listened and heard them; so a book of remembrance was written before Him for those who fear the Lord and who meditate on His name. . . .*

> *Then you shall again discern between the righteous and the wicked, between one who serves God and one who does not serve Him.*⁵⁹

---

⁵⁷ Proverbs 19:17; Proverbs 28:27 ("He who gives to the poor will not lack, but he who hides his eyes will have many curses.").

⁵⁸ Numbers 22:22–33.

⁵⁹ Malachi 3:13–18.

God created a book of remembrance not for His sake, but for the sake of His people. He created the book of remembrance to meet the cry that justice is not rewarded on the earth.

B. God's Justice includes judgment and reward

Justice is defined by why God created the book of remembrance. Justice requires the outcome of evil to be remembered as well as punishing it. Justice is also defined by good being rewarded as such.

God's book of remembrance for His people is explained in the promise that, "God will bring every deed into judgment, including every hidden thing, whether it is good or evil."[60] "For the Lord does not see as man sees; for man looks at the outward appearance, but the Lord looks at the heart."[61] Justice is defined by the promise that there will be judgment of all behavior and the heart behind all behavior. That judgment occurs at the seat of Jesus, His Son.

"For we must all appear before the judgment seat of Christ, that each one may receive the things *done* in the body, according to what he has done, whether good or bad."[62] The body being referred to is what Christians do in life.

Jesus said, "I say to you that for every idle word men may speak, they will give account of it in the day of judgment."[63]

Jesus "will both bring to light the hidden things of darkness and reveal the counsels of the hearts. Then each one's praise will come from God."[64]

Justice is defined by the fact and promise that the judgment of Christ is not blind to small acts of service. Jesus Himself said, "Whoever gives you a cup of water to drink in

---

[60] Ecclesiastes 12:14.
[61] 1 Samuel 16:7.
[62] 2 Corinthians 5:10.
[63] Matthew 12:36.
[64] 1 Corinthians 4:5.

My name because you belong to Christ, assuredly, I say to you, he will by no means lose his reward."[65]

Note the qualifier Jesus used. He said, "whoever gives … in My Name." It's not the action, but the motive behind the action that is judged. Jesus explained that the rewards of heaven are not for superficial acts of service. He said the kingdom of heaven is for the one "who does the will of My Father in heaven."[66]

Jesus explains that justice is defined not by what is done but why it is done. Justice is concerned with motive as well as action. God said, "I look upon the heart."

It's within this context that Jesus said, not everyone who claims their actions were done in His name will find reward. In explaining why, Jesus said He will say to many who cry out, "We did all these things for you" that His answer will be, "I never knew you; depart from Me, you who practice lawlessness!"[67] Acts not done in the name of Jesus for His glory are acts of lawlessness.[68] Putting God's name on an act does not change the nature of the act done in pride, arrogance, or enjoyment of power.[69] As Jesus said,

> *Woe to you, scribes and Pharisees, hypocrites! For you are like whitewashed tombs which indeed appear beautiful outwardly, but inside are full of dead men's bones and all uncleanness. Even so you also outwardly appear righteous to men, but inside you are full of hypocrisy and lawlessness.*[70]

---

[65] Mark 9:41.

[66] Matthew 12:50.

[67] Matthew 7:23.

[68] Lawlessness is defined by the motivation behind an action. As Isaiah wrote, "these people draw near with their mouths And honor Me with their lips, But have removed their hearts far from Me" (Isaiah 23:13).

[69] See generally, Matthew 24.

[70] Matthew 24:27–28.

Under God's justice, if you do right and act right, you will be rewarded. "Do not be deceived, God is not mocked; for whatever a man sows, that he will also reap."[71]

Justice is defined by the promise that there will be a day when each person individually will answer for what they have done. The book of remembrance reflects God's justice, and it provides solace and assurance that good will not be forgotten and evil will be punished. Justice promises that on that day of recompense, none will escape and "the dead, small and great, standing before God" will answer for what they have done. The book of remembrance will be opened, and then both the small and great will be "judged, each one according to his works."[72]

If justice is required on earth, justice is done in heaven. The judgment seat of Christ is about receiving justice for acts done, but getting to His seat is about salvation. The former is about what the specific individual did; the latter is about what Jesus did.

Christ judging His own occurs at His judgment seat, but the judgment at the white throne occurs in the face of God for those who reject Jesus.[73]

The adjudication at the judgment seat of Christ will result in either the verdict "Well done my good and faithful servant" or will result in the verdict of being cast out into the outer darkness with "weeping and gnashing of teeth." The former is the enjoyment of being at the wedding feast of Christ, and the latter is being found at the party without an appropriate wedding robe and being cast out of the party[74] and being forced to watch it from the outside.

Jesus explained the distinction in a parable describing what heaven was like.

> *So those servants went out into the highways and gathered together all whom they found, both bad*

---

71 Galatians 6:7.
72 Revelation 20:12–13.
73 John 5:24–30; Revelation 20:7–13.
74 Matthew 22:1–14.

*and good. And the wedding hall was filled with
guests.*

*But when the king came in to see the guests, he saw
a man there who did not have on a wedding garment. So he said to him, 'Friend, how did you come
in here without a wedding garment?' And he was
speechless. Then the king said to the servants, 'Bind
him hand and foot, take him away, and cast him
into outer darkness; there will be weeping and
gnashing of teeth.'*[75]

The justice of the judgment seat of Christ occurs *after* salvation, which is being invited and accepting the invitation to
the wedding hall which is heaven. But being allowed to enjoy the party in heaven requires having a proper wedding
garment, which is a reward due to what you have done. The
proper wedding garment is "fine linen, clean and bright, for
the fine linen is the righteous acts of the saints."[76]

Jesus used the phrase "weeping and gnashing of teeth" to
describe both the consequences of being a "wicked, lazy servant"[77] to Christ and the regret and sorrow of that servant
resulting from the missing of rewards that could have been.[78]
Both occur in heaven.[79]

Jesus made clear that in the kingdom of heaven there are
rewards and judgment on actions. When Peter asked Jesus to
His face, what do we get for giving up all and following you,
Jesus had an answer. He said,

*Assuredly, I say to you, there is no one who has left
house or brothers or sisters or father or mother or
wife or children or lands, for My sake and the
gospel's, who shall not receive a hundredfold now*

---

[75] Matthew 22:10–13.

[76] Revelation 19:8.

[77] Matthew 25:26.

[78] Luke 13:28; Matthew 8:12; Matthew 24:51; Matthew 25:30;
Matthew 22:13; Matthew 13:42.

[79] See generally, Arlen L Chitwood, *Judgment Seat of Christ*, Lamp
Broadcast Inc, (2021) at 257-274.

*in this time—houses and brothers and sisters and
mothers and children and lands, with persecu-
tions—and in the age to come, eternal life.*[80]

Justice by its nature and by its definition includes rewards
for honest work done. As Paul wrote,

*I have fought the good fight, I have finished the
race, I have kept the faith. Finally, there is laid up
for me the crown of righteousness, which the Lord,
the righteous Judge, will give to me on that Day,
and not to me only but also to all who have loved
His appearing.*[81]

Justice requires that a person gets what he has coming, both
rewards and consequences.

When Jesus explained justice, He said, "the kingdom of
heaven is like"[82] an owner who receives reports from his
servants regarding the talents he gave them to use. When the
servant with five talents returned ten and the servant with
two returned four, both were told they were good and faithful
servants and both were told, "I will make you ruler over
many things. Enter into the joy of your lord."[83] But the one
servant said I was scared and I did nothing with the talents
you gave me. God cursed him as lazy and banished him. Jesus then said when all are judged for what they did and did
not do with what was given to him by God, there "will weeping and gnashing of teeth."[84] Justice requires just deserts,
and God will meet that requirement.

It was within the context of Jesus telling this story of the
talents that He said that when the books are opened, and the
works of each person are reviewed, the judge will have a
practical test. The judge will say,

---

[80] Mark 10:29–30.
[81] 2 Timothy 4: 7–8.
[82] Matthew 25:14.
[83] Matthew 25:21.
[84] Matthew 25:30.

> *Come, you blessed of My Father, inherit the king-*
> *dom prepared for you from the foundation of the*
> *world: for I was hungry, and you gave Me food; I*
> *was thirsty, and you gave Me drink; I was a*
> *stranger, and you took Me in; I was naked, and you*
> *clothed Me; I was sick, and you visited Me; I was in*
> *prison, and you came to Me.*[85]

Justice, defined by the eye of God, includes the question—did you do justice to the weak? Did you do evil when you were strong? Did you defend the oppressed?

Jesus explained this when He told the story of the beggar Lazarus and the rich man. Jesus said Lazarus was taken to Abraham's bosom, which represents heaven, and the rich man died and suffered "torments in Hades," which represents hell.[86] When the rich man cried out in sorrow, Abraham answered him and said to him, "Son, remember that in your lifetime you received your good things, and likewise Lazarus evil things; but now he is comforted, and you are tormented."[87]

The implication was that the rich man did nothing to help Lazarus when he was tormented on earth. The rich man enjoyed his power and privilege without concern for Lazarus. Now Lazarus was in heaven and receiving blessings and happiness that he had been deprived of when on earth. The rich man, who received wealth and power and the ability to do good, but did nothing but enjoyed his place of privilege, was now left to suffer his punishment.

Solomon said, "Money answers everything,"[88] but Jesus warned of seeking only the rewards of money in life and

---

[85] Matthew 25:34–36. See also Matthew 25:37–40 ("Then the righteous will answer Him, saying, 'Lord, when did we see You hungry and feed You, or thirsty and give You drink? When did we see You a stranger and take You in, or naked and clothe You? Or when did we see You sick, or in prison, and come to You?' And the King will answer and say to them, 'Assuredly, I say to you, inasmuch as you did it to one of the least of these My brethren, you did it to Me.'").

[86] Luke 16:22–23.

[87] Luke 16:25.

[88] Ecclesiastes 10:19.

said, "For what will it profit a man if he gains the whole world, and loses his own soul?"[89]

Success is relative but it is also temporary. Stories are told that when Roman conquers were receiving praise as they walked through adoring crowds, they were told by a slave who walked with them, "remember you are a man" and "all glory is fleeting."[90] And throughout the Bible, it is observed that life is like a vapor and is fleeting.[91]

And specifically throughout the book of Ecclesiastes, King Solomon warns the successful man that in the end his pursuit of wealth and success is vanity.

> *As he came from his mother's womb, naked shall he return, To go as he came; And he shall take nothing from his labor Which he may carry away in his hand.*
>
> ...
>
> *There is an evil which I have seen under the sun, and it is common among men: A man to whom God has given riches and wealth and honor, so that he lacks nothing for himself of all he desires; yet God does not give him power to eat of it.*[92]

Paul gave a similar warning.

> *For we brought nothing into this world, and it is certain we can carry nothing out. And having food and clothing, with these we shall be content. But those who desire to be rich fall into temptation and a snare, and into many foolish and harmful lusts*

[89] Mark 8:38.

[90] Lindsay Powell, *Eager for glory: The untold story of Drusus the Elder, conqueror of Germania.* Grub Street Publishers, (2013) at 9 and *Patton*, directed by Franklin J. Schaffner, written by Francis Ford Coppola and Edmund H. North, featuring George C. Scott (Los Angeles: 20th Century Fox, 1970).

[91] Isaiah 40:8; James 4:14; 1 Peter 1:24; Psalm 39:4–5; 2 Peter 3: 10–11.

[92] Ecclesiastes 5:15; Ecclesiastes 6:1–2.

> *which drown men in destruction and perdition. For*
> *the love of money is a root of all kinds of evil, for*
> *which some have strayed from the faith in their*
> *greediness, and pierced themselves through with*
> *many sorrows.*[93]

Job after having all and losing all said, "Naked came I out of my mother's womb, and naked shall I return thither: the Lord gave, and the Lord hath taken away; blessed be the name of the Lord."[94]

The point of the story of Lazarus is God will equalize the power of the small and great at His throne. God's justice is unique in that all will be accounted for before His thrown when the book of remembrance is opened.

The book of remembrance of God is written so that mankind will know that justice does not forget the doing of good, nor does it ignore the performance of evil. God's justice says, "Whatever a man sows, that he will also reap," because "God is not unjust to forget your work and labor of love which you have shown toward His name."[95]

Justice is receiving one's reward as well as receiving what has been promised. "God is not a man, that He should lie."[96] As God promised Abraham that his descendants would have the land of Canaan,[97] his descendants, in the days of Joshua, received all that God had promised.[98] The goal of justice, reflecting the hand of God, is that "the righteous shall flourish . . . to declare that the Lord is upright; He is my rock, and there is no unrighteousness in Him."[99]

Because "the judgments of God are true and righteous altogether,"[100] David said God is not blind to evil, nor will evil prevail in the end:

---

[93]   1 Timothy 6:7–10.
[94]   Job 1:21 (KJV).
[95]   Galatians 6:7; Hebrews 6:10.
[96]   Numbers 23:19.
[97]   Genesis 15:18–21.
[98]   Joshua 21:43–45.
[99]   Psalm 92:12, 15.
[100] Psalm 19:9.

*Behold, the wicked brings forth iniquity; yes, he
conceives trouble and brings forth falsehood. He
made a pit and dug it out, and has fallen into the
ditch which he made. His trouble shall return upon
his own head, and his violent dealing shall come
down on his own crown.*[101]

Justice, by definition, recognizes evil and injustice, and the
Bible makes clear that the Law defines both and requires
recompense for each.

C. God's Justice governs kings[102] so that oppression may not reign on the earth

Returning to the operationalization of justice in a society, the
requirements of justice and the rule of law—first and fore-
most—apply to its leaders. "A ruler who lacks understanding
is a great oppressor."[103] This is made clear by many of the
Old Testament prophets in the days of ancient Israel.

The prophets to the kings of Israel asserted that there
would be judgment on those leaders who were unjust. When
God looked at the actions of King Manasseh, who reintro-
duced the abominations that his father removed from the
kingdom of Judah,[104] and at the actions of the people of Judah as a whole, who adopted those abominations, God
spoke, and Jeremiah recorded judgment against the kingdom
of Judah.

*Then the Lord said to me, "Even if Moses and
Samuel stood before Me, My mind would not be*

---

[101] Psalm 7:14–16.

[102] Psalm 72:1("Give the king your justice, O God, and your righteousness to the royal son! May he judge your people with righteousness, and your poor with justice!") (ESV); Proverbs 21:1–3
("The king's heart is in the hand of the Lord, Like the rivers of
water; He turns it wherever He wishes.").

[103] Proverbs 28:16.

[104] 2 Kings 21:1–18.

*favorable toward this people. Cast them out of My
sight, and let them go forth. And it shall be, if they
say to you, 'Where should we go?' then you shall
tell them, 'Thus says the Lord: Such as are for
death . . . the sword . . . famine . . . captivity.'"*[105]

God literally told them they could go to hell!

This is what happened under King Zedekiah[106] when King
Nebuchadnezzar invaded and conquered Judah under the
approval and judgment of God.[107] They had consistently rejected God and ignored His pleas for repentance and warn-
ings of punishment for injustice and corruption.[108]

God's plea for justice in the kingdom of Judah was delivered to three successive kings before the fall of Judah under
King Zedekiah. Jeremiah, during the reign of Zedekiah, said
to Zedekiah what God had commanded regarding justice:

*Thus says the Lord: "Go down to the house of the
king of Judah, and there speak this word, and say,
'Hear the word of the Lord, O king of Judah, you
who sit on the throne of David, you and your servants and your people who enter these gates! Thus
says the Lord: "Execute judgment and righteousness, and deliver the plundered out of the hand
of the oppressor. Do no wrong and do no violence
to the stranger, the fatherless, or the widow, nor
shed innocent blood in this place. For if you indeed
do this thing, then shall enter the gates of this
house, riding on horses and in chariots, accompa-
nied by servants and people, kings who sit on the
throne of David. But if you will not hear these
words, I swear by Myself," says the Lord, "that this
house shall become a desolation."'"*

. . . .

[105] Jeremiah 15:1–2.
[106] 2 Kings 25:1–9.
[107] Jeremiah 25:1, 9, 11; 27:1–2, 5–8.
[108] 2 Chronicles 36:15–16.

"Shall you reign because you enclose yourself in cedar? Did not your father eat and drink, and do justice and righteousness? Then it was well with him. He judged the cause of the poor and needy; then it was well. Was not this knowing Me?" says the Lord. "Yet your eyes and your heart are for nothing but your covetousness, for shedding innocent blood, and practicing oppression and violence."[109]

God defined justice as executing righteousness, delivering the plundered out of the hand of the oppressor, doing no wrong or violence to the stranger, the fatherless, or the widow, nor shedding innocent blood. God judged Judah for violating these principles.

To defend His judgment, God challenged His prophet Jeremiah, saying, "Roam back and forth through the streets of Jerusalem, and look now and take note. And look in her open squares to see if you can find a man [as Abraham sought in Sodom], one who is just, who [has integrity and moral courage and] seeks truth (faithfulness)." God said if you find one, "Then I will pardon Jerusalem—[for the sake of one uncompromisingly righteous person]."[110]

With Jeremiah finding none, God concluded, "They do not plead the cause, the cause of the fatherless; yet they prosper, and the right of the needy they do not defend. . . . The prophets prophesy falsely, and the priests rule by their own power; and My people love to have it so."[111]

God defines injustice as not only doing evil, but knowingly doing so. An unjust society is not only led by kings and leaders and judges who do not protect the weak and the poor and the stranger and the widow, but God defines an unjust society as one that enjoys and supports such behavior by those who rule.

---

[109] Jeremiah 22:1–5, 15–17.
[110] Jeremiah 5:1 (AMP).
[111] Jeremiah 5:28, 31.

Justice is defined by what the people want, as well as what they do. The kingdom of Israel, after the reign of David beginning with Solomon, ignored doing justice for generations of kings. The stories and consequences of their disobedience is what is encompassed in the books of the Bible, from Judges through Malachi.

Because of the sins of the sons of King David, the kingdom of Israel was divided into the Northern Kingdom and the kingdom of Judah,[112] both of which continued to reject God. In both kingdoms, God found injustice at the hands of those who ruled and governed under the Law of Moses.

God requires those who have lawful authority to act justly, as He acts justly. During the seventy years of Babylonian captivity, God commanded the dispossessed inhabitants of Judah to do justice and, through the Prophet Ezekiel, said, when they are restored, "My princes shall no more oppress My people . . . Thus says the Lord God: 'Enough, O princes of Israel! Remove violence and plundering, execute justice and righteousness, and stop dispossessing My people,' says the Lord God. You shall have honest scales, an honest ephah, and an honest bath."[113]

Again, God made clear that justice is what He seeks in the land of men and that justice is defined by how the law is applied. Injustice is defined, in part, by the powerful using their position to dispossess and plunder the weak. To those who do injustice, who say God does not see, justice responds, evil does not escape the eyes or judgment of God.[114]

Because the kingdom of Judah had fallen into deep treachery and injustice before God, God allowed the destruction of Judah by allowing King Nebuchadnezzar of Babylon—modern-day northern Saudi Arabia, Iraq, Syria, and southern

[112] 2 Kings 17:20–23.
[113] Ezekiel 45:8–10.
[114] Ezekiel 8:12.

Turkey—to attack and destroy the kingdom in 597 BC.[115] It was this destruction that led to the stories of Daniel as well as Shadrach, Meshach, and Abednego and the story of Esther.

The Northern Kingdom of Israel fared no better, for it too was corrupt. God sent the prophet Hosea to the king and relayed the same indictment that was laid against the kingdom of Judah:

> *Hear the word of the Lord, you children of Israel,*
> *for the Lord brings a charge against the inhabitants*
> *of the land:*
>
> *There is no truth or mercy or knowledge of God in*
> *the land. By swearing and lying, killing and steal-*
> *ing and committing adultery, they break all re-*
> *straint, with bloodshed upon bloodshed. Therefore*
> *the land will mourn; and everyone who dwells there*
> *will waste away with the beasts of the field and the*
> *birds of the air; even the fish of the sea will be tak-*
> *en away.*[116]

As with the kingdom of Judah, God allowed an enemy of Israel, the Assyrians—modern-day northern Iraq, northwestern Iran, southeastern Turkey, and eastern Syria—to destroy the kingdom in 722 BC as a consequence of their committing injustice and abominations before God.[117]

The Bible defines justice by what behavior God rejects as well as what behavior He advocates. In both the kingdoms of Judah and Israel, injustice was found because people were covetous; they shed innocent blood; they practiced oppression and violence; they committed perjury, stole, and committed adultery as a way of life with no regard to the laws of

---

[115] 2 Chronicles 36:11–21. See also 2 Kings 25:1–21, for a discussion on the fall of Judah, the blinding of Zedekiah, the killing of his sons, and the carrying away of the Jewish captives to Babylon.

[116] Hosea 4:1–3 (internal quotation mark omitted).

[117] 2 Kings 17:1–2, 6–7, 9, 13–18.

God.[118] In Judah, they did business by evoking the name of the Lord, but they actually swore and dealt falsely.[119] They broke the Law of Moses that commanded that, "You shall not steal, nor deal falsely, nor lie to one another. And you shall not swear by My name falsely, nor shall you profane the name of your God: I *am* the Lord."[120]

The prophet Isaiah tried to warn the kingdom of Judah that injustice does not escape the eyes of God and that they needed to change. He decried how the city of Jerusalem had fallen into evil:

> *How the faithful city has become a harlot! It was full of justice; righteousness lodged in it, But now murderers. . . . Your princes are rebellious and companions of thieves; everyone loves bribes, and follows after rewards. They do not defend the fatherless, nor does the cause of the widow come before them."[121]*

Jesus Himself cried out,

> *"O Jerusalem, Jerusalem, the one who kills the prophets and stones those who are sent to her! How often I wanted to gather your children together, as a hen gathers her chicks under her wings, but you were not willing!"[122]*

But His tears did not prevent Him from stating that justice would come to her because of her evil and abandonment of God.

> *Now as He drew near, He saw the city and wept over it, saying, "If you had known, even you, especially in this your day, the things that make for your peace! But now they are hidden from your eyes. For*

---

[118] Isaiah 5:20–21; 10:1–3; 59:15.
[119] Jeramiah 5:2.
[120] Leviticus 19:11–12.
[121] Isaiah 1:21–23.
[122] Matthew 23:37.

days will come upon you when your enemies will build an embankment around you, surround you and close you in on every side, and level you, and your children within you, to the ground; and they will not leave in you one stone upon another, because you did not know the time of your visitation."[123]

But they were insistent, demanding with loud voices that He be crucified. And the voices of these men and of the chief priests prevailed.

... Now as they led Him away... a great multitude of the people followed Him, and women who also mourned and lamented Him. But Jesus, turning to them, said, "Daughters of Jerusalem, do not weep for Me, but weep for yourselves and for your children. For indeed the days are coming in which they will say, 'Blessed are the barren, wombs that never bore, and breasts which never nursed!' Then they will begin 'to say to the mountains, "Fall on us!" and to the hills, "Cover us!"' For if they do these things in the green wood, what will be done in the dry?"[124]

"See! Your house is left to you desolate; for I say to you, you shall see Me no more till you say, 'Blessed is He who comes in the name of the Lord!'"[125]

In 70 AD, the word of Jesus was fulfilled.

The prophet Isaiah defined justice by the example of what he found lacking in Judah. Justice in the eyes of God is honesty and fidelity in those who rule and those who are ruled. God requires that societies "learn to do good; seek justice, rebuke the oppressor; defend the fatherless, [and] plead for the widow."[126] From the days of Moses, God required these

---

[123] Luke 19:41–44.
[124] Luke 23:23–31.
[125] Matthew 23:38–39.
[126] Isaiah 1:17.

things of His people, so they would be an example of justice. As God commanded Moses to say to His people,

> *You shall not oppress a hired servant who is poor and needy, whether one of your brethren or one of the aliens who is in your land within your gates. Each day you shall give him his wages, and not let the sun go down on it, for he is poor and has set his heart on it; lest he cry out against you to the Lord, and it be sin to you.*[127]

Israel was to reflect the example God set by His own actions. "For the Lord your God is God of gods and Lord of lords, the great God, mighty and awesome, who shows no partiality nor takes a bribe. He administers justice for the fatherless and the widow, and loves the stranger, giving him food and clothing. Therefore love the stranger, for you were strangers in the land of Egypt."[128]

God instructed Israel that justice is defined by the reciprocity of the justice God showed them when they were helpless.

> *And if a stranger dwells with you in your land, you shall not mistreat him. The stranger who dwells among you shall be to you as one born among you, and you shall love him as yourself; for you were strangers in the land of Egypt: I am the Lord your God.*

> *You shall do no injustice in judgment, in measurement of length, weight, or volume. You shall have honest scales [and] honest weights . . . I am the Lord your God, who brought you out of the land of Egypt.*[129]

---

[127] Deuteronomy 24:14–15.
[128] Deuteronomy 10:17–19.
[129] Leviticus 19:33–36 (internal quotation marks omitted).

3.
I, the Lord, Will Put My Laws in Their Minds[1] and Will Separate Your Sins from You,[2] and I Will Remember Your Sins No More[3]

God's justice is about truth, but God's justice is also about reconciliation, even when punishment is required. As Solomon observed, "One who turns away his ear from hearing the law, even his prayer, is an abomination."[4] He also observed, "Because of the transgression of a land" government is instituted in "princes" and those princes, like all men, should be "of understanding and knowledge" so that justice "will be prolonged" on the earth. [5]

Although God recognizes right and punishes wrong and unfairness,[6] God's justice is also merciful and seeks to show mercy. As David prayed, "Do not remember the sins of my youth nor my transgressions; according to Your mercy, remember me."[7]

God's justice acknowledges the difference between the person and what a person does. David cried out to God, saying, see me as me; do not see my sin and define me by my

---

[1] Jeremiah 31:33; Hebrews 8:10 (NIV).
[2] Psalms 103:12.
[3] Jeremiah 31:34; Hebrews 8:12.
[4] Proverbs 28:9.
[5] Proverbs 28:2.
[6] Exodus 22:21–24, 27.
[7] Psalm 25:7.

sin. David wrote that the Lord heard his prayer. He wrote, "I know that the Lord saves His anointed; He will answer him from His holy heaven with the saving strength of His right hand."[8]

The justice of God does not define a person by his worst bad day; God sees a person by the wholeness of who that person is. God honors the prayer, "According to Your mercy remember me."

Justice is about defining "ought" and "ought not," while law is about what shall be required. The Old Testament is thought to be about the wrath of God on the evil of man and that the wicked will not escape the punishment of the almighty God.

But God's justice is not solely about punishment; it's also about rectification. The Old Testament is a story of God finding ways to apply His justice rather than His wrath. Even before the advent of the Law of Moses, God applied justice to the nations. Even the great story of God's wrath upon Sodom and Gomorrah is a story of God seeking to be just.

Genesis records that God, with two of His angels, visited His friend Abraham to tell him that in one year he would have a son, Isaac.[9] Before He left, God discussed with Abraham His plans to punish Sodom and Gomorrah:

> And the Lord said, "Shall I hide from Abraham
> what I am doing, since Abraham shall surely be-
> come a great and mighty nation, and all the nations
> of the earth shall be blessed in him? For I have
> known him, in order that he may command his chil-
> dren and his household after him, that they keep the
> way of the Lord, to do righteousness and justice,
> that the Lord may bring to Abraham what He has
> spoken to him." And the Lord said, "Because the
> outcry against Sodom and Gomorrah is great, and
> because their sin is very grave, I will go down now
> and see whether they have done altogether accord-

---

8   Psalm 20:6. See also Psalm 18:46–49.
9   Genesis 18:10.

*ing to the outcry against it that has come to Me;
and if not, I will know."*[10]

Note that the law is not abridged. The sin of Sodom and Gomorrah was not whitewashed. God said they were so evil that He Himself would deal with it. But the sin of Sodom and Gomorrah is not what led to its destruction. God found a way to save the city. As Genesis records,

Then the men turned away from there and went toward Sodom, but Abraham still stood before the Lord. And Abraham came near and said, "Would You also destroy the righteous with the wicked? Suppose there were fifty righteous within the city; would You also destroy the place and not spare it for the fifty righteous that were in it? Far be it from You to do such a thing as this, to slay the righteous with the wicked, so that the righteous should be as the wicked; far be it from You! Shall not the Judge of all the earth do right?"[11]

Here is how God found a way to save the city. He knew that Abraham would advocate for the city by appealing to His heart of mercy and grace. Abraham would appeal to His justice.

Abraham said, "Would You also destroy the place and not spare it for the fifty righteous that were in it? . . . Far be it from You to do such a thing as this, to slay the righteous with the wicked."[12]

God answered this appeal to His justice:

So the Lord said, "If I find in Sodom fifty righteous within the city, then I will spare all the place for their sakes." Then Abraham answered and said, "Indeed now, I who am but dust and ashes, have taken it upon myself to speak to the Lord: Suppose

---

[10] Genesis 18:17–21.
[11] Genesis 18:22–25.
[12] Genesis 18:23–25.

> *there were five less than the fifty righteous; would*
> *You destroy all of the city for lack of five?" So He*
> *said, "If I find there forty-five, I will not destroy it."*
> *And he spoke to Him yet again and said, "Suppose*
> *there should be forty found there?" So He said, "I*
> *will not do it for the sake of forty." Then he said,*
> *"Let not the Lord be angry, and I will speak: Sup-*
> *pose thirty should be found there?" So He said, "I*
> *will not do it if I find thirty there." And he said,*
> *"Indeed now, I have taken it upon myself to speak*
> *to the Lord: Suppose twenty should be found*
> *there?" So He said, "I will not destroy it for the*
> *sake of twenty." Then he said, "Let not the Lord be*
> *angry, and I will speak but once more: Suppose ten*
> *should be found there?" And He said, "I will not*
> *destroy it for the sake of ten." So the Lord went His*
> *way as soon as He had finished speaking with*
> *Abraham; and Abraham returned to his place.*[13]

This is the justice of God. He would let this famously sinful city exist in all its sin if He found ten righteous people. For their sake, the city would flourish.

The city of Sodom and Gomorrah was destroyed, not because of their sins, but because the angels of the Lord barely found one righteous man in the city when they were looking for ten.[14]

So much for the biblical heresy made by American social conservative television evangelists who posit that if America is not punished for her sins, God will have to apologize to Sodom and Gomorrah!

Such statements are heresy regarding the justice of God. First, in His perfection, God does not need to apologize for anything He does or does not do.

Second, as far as comparisons go, surely there are more than ten righteous people living in America and more than

---

[13] Genesis 18:26–33.
[14] Genesis 19:12–27.

one righteous man asking for intercession for her before God's mercy seat.

Lastly, it would be better for American social conservative Christians to honor God's Word that says, "If my people . . . will humble themselves, and pray and . . . turn from their wicked ways, then I will . . . forgive their sin and heal their land."[15]

Perhaps if social conservative television evangelists complied with the admonition that, "If my people . . . will humble themselves, and pray and . . . turn from *their* wicked ways"—and spent more time praying for America and manifesting the miracles of the New Testament and less time complaining about her sins and praying for her punishment—God's promise, "I will . . . heal their land" would be seen in America.

As to the sins of a nation, Jesus said of Sodom and Gomorrah, if the miracles He performed had been seen in her, she would have repented.[16] Consider the significance of Jesus comparing Sodom and Gomorrah to the nation of Israel. Jesus said to the chosen people of God that had the great city of sin seen what He had done before them, that sinful city would have repented and accepted Him. But His chosen people were rejecting God standing before them in the flesh.

God's justice includes the adjudication of right over wrong and the application of fair judgment. All true. But Jesus came to show God's justice is defined by love, mercy and grace:

> *Now it came to pass . . . they entered a village of the Samaritans . . . But they did not receive Him . . .*
> *And when His disciples James and John saw this, they said, "Lord, do You want us to command fire to come down from heaven and consume them, just as Elijah did?"*

---

[15] 2 Chronicles 7:14.
[16] See Matthew 11:20, 23.

77

> *But He turned and rebuked them, and said, "You
> do not know what manner of spirit you are of. For
> the Son of Man did not come to destroy men's lives,
> but to save them." And they went to another
> village.*[17]

Jesus rebuked them because of their desire to see the judgment of God fall on the heads of others was about self-righteous pride, not the righteousness of God or His judgments.

Fortunately, God's ways are higher than those of self-serving and prideful religious leaders, which have existed both before and after the time of Jesus. It should not be forgotten that it was such priests who conspired to kill Jesus and delivered Him to the Romans to be crucified on the cross on false criminal charges. It was religious men who raised a lynch mob in the court of Pontius Pilate, demanding a guilty man go free in order to kill an innocent one.

The distinction between justice in the hands of the mob compared to justice in the hand of God includes God providing time for repentance and providing a way for repentance and restoration to occur.[18] "Those who will not deliver themselves into the hand of God's mercy cannot be delivered out of the hand of His justice."[19]

In the face of God's judgment David cried out, "I am in great distress. Please let us fall into the hand of the Lord, for His mercies are great; but do not let me fall into the hand of

---

[17] Luke 9:51–56.

[18] See the story of Joab and how he got David to forgive Absalom by appealing to David's sense of justice. Joab had a woman pretend to being a widow and she begged David to spear her son's life when her son was guilty of murder and rightly being subject to the death penalty. When David ordered clemency for the woman's son from the penalty of death, Joab had her say why do you not do this for Absalom. Then David spared his life. 2 Samuel 14.

[19] Matthew Henry, *Mathew Henry's Commentary on the Bible*, Hosea, Chapter Two, Verses 6–13.

man."[20] When David repented in the face of God's judgment and punishment, "the Lord relented from the destruction, and said to the angel who was destroying the people, 'It is enough; now restrain your hand.'"[21]

God allows man to see the evil in his sin and seek God for forgiveness. This allowance of time creates complaints that God is slow in applying justice to those who do evil and disregard His law. This complaint is not new. To the complaints of the early Christian church regarding the failure of God to fulfill His promises regarding the return of Christ, Peter answered,

> *The Lord does not delay [as though He were unable to act] and is not slow about His promise, as some count slowness, but is [extraordinarily] patient toward you, not wishing for any to perish, but for all to come to repentance."[22]*

Justice in the hand of God is defined by the goal of rectification through grace and mercy. As Paul wrote, justice has a particular perspective:

> *I urge . . . prayers, intercessions . . . for kings and all who are in [positions of] high authority . . . This [kind of praying] is good and acceptable and pleasing in the sight of God our Savior, who wishes all people . . . to come to the knowledge and recognition of the [divine] truth. For there is [only] one God, and [only] one Mediator between God and mankind, the Man Christ Jesus, who gave Himself as a ransom [a substitutionary sacrifice to atone] for all, the testimony given at the right and proper time.[23]*

---

[20] 2 Samuel 24:14.
[21] 2 Samuel 24:16.
[22] 2 Peter 3:9 (AMP).
[23] 1 Timothy 2:1–6 (AMP).

With this point in mind, the significance of the story of Sodom and Gomorrah is that the wrath of God can be stayed by the prayers and appeals of one man.[24] God's wrath can be stayed by reasoned prayer based on His promise of justice over His application of the harshness of the Law.

Both Isaiah and Jeremiah wrote that God's true heart and goal regarding the Law was providing redemption and mercy upon cries for help.

> *I, even I, am He who blots out your transgressions for My own sake; and I will not remember your sins. Put Me in remembrance; let us contend to-gether; state your case, that you may be acquitted."[25]*

> *But I called on your name, Lord, from deep within the pit. You heard me when I cried, 'Listen to my pleading! Hear my cry for help!' Yes, you came when I called; you told me, 'Do not fear.' Lord, you have come to my defense; you have redeemed my life.[26]*

In the face of mercy and grace, one could ask, is the Law of an eye for an eye, judgment, and the wrath of God and punishment for evil made of no effect by mercy and grace? First, it should be understood that although the requirement of an eye for an eye carried a connotation about God's vengeance against evil, it was actually a law of proportionality.

Under God's justice, if a person took your eye, you only had a right to take the eye of the aggressor and no more. This prevented the rise of blood feuds and guaranteed equal punishment. To the question of God's wrath and judgment, in the face of mercy and grace, the answer is found in observation

---

[24] James 5:16; 2 Chronicles 7:14.
[25] Isaiah 43:25–26.
[26] Lamentations 3:55-58 (NLT).

that God's judgment, though stayed by His mercy,[27] is not stayed forever.[28]

Mercy and grace do not disregard their sister, the law, and the presence of justice does not mean the lack of enforcement of the law. After God gave the children of Israel the Ten Commandments, the incident of the golden calf occurred. Upon seeing Israel's disobedience, Exodus records:

> *And the Lord said to Moses, "Go, get down! For your people whom you brought out of the land of Egypt have corrupted themselves. They have turned aside quickly out of the way which I commanded them. They have made themselves a molded calf, and worshiped it and sacrificed to it, and said, 'This is your god, O Israel, that brought you out of the land of Egypt!'" And the Lord said to Moses, "I have seen this people, and indeed it is a stiff-necked people! Now, therefore, let Me alone, that My wrath may burn hot against them and I may consume them. And I will make of you a great nation."[29]*

As both Cain and Abraham did, Moses appealed the ruling of God under the Law and pled for clemency under God's mercy:

> *"Lord, why does Your wrath burn hot against Your people, whom You have brought out of the land of Egypt with great power and with a mighty hand? Why should the Egyptians speak, and say, 'He brought them out to harm them, to kill them in the mountains, and to consume them from the face of the earth'? Turn from Your fierce wrath, and relent from this harm to Your people. Remember Abraham, Isaac, and Israel, Your servants, to whom You*

---

[27] See generally Psalm 103, for a discussion on the nature of God and His mercy.

[28] See Amos 1:11 (NIV); Psalm 103:9 (NIV); Revelation 6:10–17 (NIV).

[29] Exodus 32:7–10.

> *swore by Your own self, and said to them, 'I will*
> *multiply your descendants as the stars of heaven;*
> *and all this land that I have spoken of I give to your*
> *descendants, and they shall inherit it forever.'" So*
> *the Lord relented from the harm which He said He*
> *would do to His people.*[30]

As with Cain, as with Abraham, God granted the appeal of clemency He received at His Court of Justice. From the appeal of Moses, God did not destroy the rebellious people. But the Law is not mocked. Their crimes did not go unpunished, and God "plagued the people because of what they did with the calf which Aaron [had] made."[31]

Justice in the hand of God does include the application of retribution. After the situation with the calf, an insurrection occurred in which three leaders of the Jews rose up to challenge the leadership of Moses and Aaron. Backed by an additional 250 leaders of the people, they accused Moses of abuse of power for assuming that only he could be holy and speak for God.[32]

Justice includes governmental righteous judgment and retribution. Witnessing this mutiny and false accusation of His friend, God said to Moses and Aaron, "Separate yourselves from among this congregation, that I may consume them in a moment."[33] But Moses and Aaron again appealed to God's justice, and "they fell on their faces, and said, 'O God, the God of the spirits of all flesh, *shall one man sin, and You be angry with all the congregation?*'"[34]

Justice requires the sword of government to be tempered by the principle of proportionality. Note the substance of the appeal. They pled, as Abraham pled, before the face of God, that punishment should be proportional and specific to the

---

[30] Exodus 32:11–14.
[31] Exodus 32:35.
[32] Numbers 16:1–35.
[33] Numbers 16:20–21.
[34] Numbers 16:22 (emphasis added).

offender. The guilt of the father, under the justice of God, is not applied to the son.[35]

Heeding their appeal, God opened the earth, and the leaders of the rebellion and the 250 who followed them fell into the earth and were covered up.[36] Justice under the hand of God applies specific punishments for the specific evil done by the specific person who committed it.

After the results of the attempted coup d'état, the entire congregation of the Jews rose up the very next day against Moses and Aaron, accusing them of murder in the name of God in front of the tabernacle of God.[37] Because God knew Moses would plead for clemency for this newest crime, God did not speak to Moses, but immediately sent a plague upon the congregation with the intent to "consume them in a moment."[38] Only when Aaron ran in the midst of the congregation holding incense before God and standing "between the dead and the living" was the plague stopped.[39]

The burning incense represented praise, the promises of God, and repentance. Upon seeing it, God relented and called back the plague. Before He relented, 14,700 people were dead, in addition to the 250 who were killed the day before.[40]

Justice, when mercy and grace are applied, cannot withhold retribution demanded by their sister, the law, when the law is subsequently violated. When the children of Israel went into the land of Moab and made sacrifices to their gods, including Baal, God sent a plague into their midst. But He relented, saying to Moses, "Phinehas [the grandson of Aaron] has turned back My wrath."[41]

---

[35] Deuteronomy 24:16 ("Fathers shall not be put to death for their children, nor shall children be put to death for their fathers; a person shall be put to death for his own sin.").

[36] Numbers 16:31–33.

[37] Numbers 16:41–43.

[38] Numbers 16:45–46.

[39] Numbers 16:48.

[40] Numbers 16:49.

[41] Numbers 25:11.

This story of one man turning back the wrath of God occurred at the incident at Peor. Phinehas killed "an Israelite man [who] brought into the camp a Midianite woman right before the eyes of Moses and the whole assembly of Israel." God had commanded that all who participated in the worship of Baal were to be killed.[42]

When Aaron's grandson killed the idolater for his arrogance in bringing a woman of Baal into the camp of Israel—not to mention that the woman herself was a princess of the Midianite king—God's anger cooled, and He relented from the unleashing the plague on the entire nation.[43]

As previously noted, mercy and grace does not mean that the law is without enforcement and that there is no consequence for disobedience. God's law is truly hard and can be devastating. To purify the tribe of Levi—the servants of God in His tabernacle—of those who participated in the creation of the golden calf, three thousand men were killed. Moses commanded, "Let every man kill his brother, every man his companion, and every man his neighbor. . . . Consecrate yourselves today to the Lord, that He may bestow on you a blessing this day, for every man has opposed his son and his brother."[44]

Death was required to purify the priesthood of God's people. It was a harsh requirement of the Law, but without the cleansing, the priesthood could not act as the spiritual conduit to God, which would allow for mercy and grace to flow from God to the people.

But God's law has always been subject to His justice through grace and mercy. When Nineveh repented, "God saw their works, that they turned from their evil way; and God relented from the disaster that He had said He would bring upon them, and He did not do it."[45]

---

[42] Numbers 25:6 (NIV).
[43] Numbers 25:7–13. See also Deuteronomy 20:17–18 (NIV) (regarding God's revenge on the Midianites).
[44] Exodus 32:27–29 (internal quotation marks omitted)).
[45] See Jonah 3:10.

The law is what the law requires, but justice is what justice seeks.

The stories of Israel under Moses and Aaron are replete with retribution, but also punishment tempered by grace and mercy and reconciliation. Just as the law of thrust and lift are higher laws than the law of gravity, and the former allows a plane to fly, grace and mercy are higher than the judgment of the law. Grace and mercy allow man to live in the presence of God without fear.

God, by His behavior, establishes that grace and mercy, in the face of justice, is a higher principle than the righteous judgment of the law. When the people rebelled against Moses, God sent snakes to punish the Jews, but upon the pleas of Moses, God relented and instructed him on how to heal those who were bitten by the snakes.[46] Under the Law of Moses, through Moses himself, God always sought to temper retribution to achieve the higher levels of justice—mercy, reconciliation, and rehabilitation.

Under the Old Testament, God commanded not only that justice be done, but He also defined justice by the heart of the person who acts justly because[47] out of the heart springs the issues of life.[48] God looks at the heart of a person, the motive behind what is done. As Samuel records, "The Lord does not see as man sees; for man looks at the outward appearance, but the Lord looks at the heart." [49]

Peter warned the church, "Do not let your adornment be merely outward—arranging the hair, wearing gold, or putting on fine apparel—rather let it be the hidden person of the heart, with the incorruptible beauty of a gentle and quiet spirit, which is very precious in the sight of God."[50]

God is concerned with what is done in the secret place of the heart. Jesus explained the full nature of the Law of

---

[46] Numbers 21:4–9.
[47] Deuteronomy 15:9–10.
[48] Proverbs 4:23.
[49] 1 Samuel 16:7.
[50] 1 Peter 3:3–4.

Moses by stating that the real issue is the motive of an act of obedience, not just the act. As Jesus said,

> *"You have heard that it was said to those of old,*
> *'You shall not murder, and whoever murders will be*
> *in danger of the judgment.' But I say to you that*
> *whoever is angry with his brother without a cause*
> *shall be in danger of the judgment. . . . Agree with*
> *your adversary quickly, while you are on the way*
> *with him, lest your adversary deliver you to the*
> *judge, the judge hand you over to the officer, and*
> *you be thrown into prison. . . . You have heard*
> *that . . . 'You shall not commit adultery.' But I say*
> *to you that whoever looks at a woman to lust for*
> *her has already committed adultery with her in his*
> *heart."*[51]

Obedience to the law is not the fulfillment of justice, but the defining of justice begins with obedience to the law. Jesus said, "The scribes and the Pharisees sit in Moses's seat. Therefore whatever they tell you to observe, that observe and do,"[52] but "I say to you, that unless your righteousness exceeds the righteousness of the scribes and Pharisees, you will by no means enter the kingdom of heaven."[53]

Why did Jesus say that? Because the scribes and the Pharisees were not just; they outwardly obeyed the Law, but not the purpose of the Law. Jesus rebuked them for applying the Law above the meaning and purpose of the Law and by twisting the Law for their own purposes.[54]

Jesus complained that through their manipulation of the Law in "laying aside the commandment of God, you hold the tradition of men . . . . [thus] making the word of God of no

---

[51] Matthew 5:21–22, 25, 27–28. For a discussion of the law against adultery, see Leviticus 20:10.
[52] Matthew 23:2–3.
[53] Matthew 5:20.
[54] Mark 7:1–11.

effect through your tradition which you have handed down."[55]

Stephen came to the same conclusion, saying to the Pharisees, "You stiff-necked and uncircumcised in heart and ears! You always resist the Holy Spirit; as your fathers did, so do you. Which of the prophets did your fathers not persecute? And they killed those who foretold the coming of the Just One, of whom you now have become the betrayers and murderers, who have received the law by the direction of angels and have not kept it."[56] Jesus said the same thing.[57]

Jesus said, "Woe to you, scribes and Pharisees, hypocrites! For you pay tithe of mint and anise and cumin, and have neglected the weightier matters of the law: justice and mercy and faith. These you ought to have done, without leaving the others undone."[58]

Despising mercy and grace and only asserting the validity of the letter of law, a lawyer tested Jesus by asking what was the greatest of the Law in order to find Him guilty of blasphemy. Jesus, citing the Law of Moses,[59] answered:

> *"You shall love the Lord your God with all your heart, with all your soul, and with all your mind." This is the first and great commandment. And the second is like it: 'You shall love your neighbor as yourself.' On these two commandments hang all the Law and the Prophets.*[60]

Jesus made clear that under the eyes of God, what is required of man is that he do justice, and in so doing, the interests and purpose of the Law will be achieved.

Jesus said to His disciples on the night of His betrayal, "A new commandment I give to you, that you love one another; as I have loved you, that you also love one another. By this,

---

[55] Mark 7:8, 13.

[56] Acts 7:51–53.

[57] See Luke 11:47–51.

[58] Matthew 23:23. See also Luke 11:37–54.

[59] Deuteronomy 6:5; Leviticus 19:18.

[60] Matthew 22:37–40.

all will know that you are My disciples, if you have love for one another."[61]

Justice is not only defined by the letter of the law; it is defined by the application of mercy, grace, and love in the face of the law. Although the law is the starting point in defining justice,[62] confidence in the obedience to the law alone does not complete the definition of justice.

To show and seek mercy for others, as Matthew records, "is more than all the whole burnt offerings and sacrifices."[63] God says justice begins in the heart. Jesus expanded the Law against murder, adultery, resisting adversaries, and divorce to include the heart of these offenses, not just the act of doing these offenses.[64]

Put another way, Jesus said the violation of these offenses, in the eyes of God, is completed with the *mens rea* as well as the *actus reus* of these offenses. As Mark records, Jesus made clear that tradition and outward obedience to laws does not make a man holy. Righteousness, Jesus made clear, is what flows out of a man's heart not the outward appearance of a man's actions. "When He had called all the multitude to Himself, He said to them, 'Hear Me, everyone, and understand: There is nothing that enters a man from outside which can defile him; but the things which come out of him, those are the things that defile a man.'"[65]

Throughout the Old Testament, mercy and grace—God's justice—are shown to be higher than the requirements of the

---

[61] Mark 12:28–34; John 13:34–35.

[62] Jesus defended the existence of the Law: "Do not think that I came to destroy the Law or the Prophets. I did not come to destroy but to fulfill. For assuredly, I say to you, till heaven and earth pass away, one jot or one tittle will by no means pass from the law till all is fulfilled" (Matthew 5:17–18).

[63] Mark 12:33.

[64] Matthew 5:21–22, 27–28.

[65] Mark 7:14–15.

Law. For example, although it is written, a "Moabite shall not enter the assembly of the Lord; even to the tenth generation,"[66] the Bible itself dedicates an entire book to one Moabite woman. The Bible records that Ruth not only entered the assembly but became the great-grandmother of King David[67] and is in the recorded family line of Jesus.[68]

The book of Ruth is a story chronicling the life of a Moabite woman who suffered the death of her husband and provided for her mother-in-law.[69] Ruth followed her to a land and lived with a people that were not hers. Ruth famously said:

For wherever you go, I will go; and wherever you lodge, I will lodge; your people shall be my people, and your God, my God. Where you die, I will die, and there will I be buried. The Lord do so to me, and more also, if anything but death parts you and me.[70]

Ruth said let "the Lord do," not let God do.

When Ruth said she would stay with her mother-in-law, she invoked the protection and judgment of the Lord. "The Lord" reflects God's justice and mercy and love. She prayed, under the protection and eyes of the Lord, I will not leave you, and your people will be my people, and your God will be mine.

God said no Moabite shall be in His house. True. But God first said, honor thy mother and father, that life will be well with you.[71] In Ruth's case, under the eyes of the Lord, "all that you have done for your mother-in-law since the death of your husband, and how you have left your father and your

---

[66] Deuteronomy 23:3.
[67] Ruth 4:17 ("And they called his name Obed. He is the father of Jesse, the father of David.").
[68] Matthew 1:5.
[69] Ruth 1:16, 2:2, 6–7.
[70] Ruth 1:16–17.
[71] Exodus 20:12.

mother and the land of your birth, and have come to a people whom you did not know before"[72] was seen and known.

Under the justice of God, His command that no Moabite would be in His tabernacle was stayed, and the justice of His fifth commandment prevailed. God provided Ruth a protector who said over her, "The Lord repay your work, and a full reward be given you by the Lord God of Israel, under whose wings you have come for refuge."[73]

Under God's justice, the kings of ancient Israel were condemned for failure to care for the widow and the orphan, and from the days of Moses, God defined justice as protecting the helpless.

In the story of Ruth, God took notice of this unmarried helpless Moabite woman who was a person outside of His promises to the children of Abraham. God provided for all of her needs because she honored His law. God provided for her physical safety[74] as well as for her financial needs[75] in the land of Israel under His wings before His eyes. She sought His refuge and she received it.

The Scriptures define who God is, and He is what He does. Through His example, He requires men to do likewise—to do justly and love mercy, and to do both with humility.[76]

Another famous story of God's mercy superseding His law is the story of Rahab, who hid the spies in Jericho.[77] God commanded that nothing was to remain of the city and that all the inhabitants were to be killed. Yet, God commanded that Rahab was to be protected and welcomed into the assembly of His people because she was just to the spies.

The implementation of the law can be unjust if its implementation is cruel or unreasonable or applied without con-

---

[72] Ruth 2:11.
[73] Ruth 2:12.
[74] Ruth 2:9 ("Have I not commanded the young men not to touch you? And when you are thirsty, go to the vessels and drink from what the young men have drawn.").
[75] Ruth 2:8,15-18.
[76] Micah 6:8.
[77] Joshua 2:4–21, 6:17, 21–25.

sideration of external factors. God commanded that all who were in the city were to be killed, but Joshua said, not Rahab because she is just before the eyes of the Lord. Justice, not blind obedience, prevailed. Rahab married Salmon and would become the mother of Boaz,[78] who would marry the Moabite, Ruth. Both women are in the maternal line of David, Solomon, and Jesus.

The Law of Moses, as discussed above, had harsh commands, and in parts, God commanded that the Law should be executed and the children of Israel were to show no pity in its application. The reason for its harshness was to separate the children of Israel from the peoples of the land and to purify the land of various abominations. God used the Law of Moses and Israel to punish crimes of human sacrifice and other abominations in the eyes of God.

Moses relayed God's command, saying to the people, "Completely destroy them—the Hittites, Amorites, Canaanites, Perizzites, Hivites and Jebusites—as the Lord your God has commanded you. Otherwise, they will teach you to follow all the detestable things they do in worshiping their gods, and you will sin against the Lord your God."[79]

Later, God commanded Moses to "take vengeance on the Midianites . . . . [whose] women . . . followed Balaam's advice and enticed the Israelites to be unfaithful to the Lord in the Peor incident so that a plague struck the Lord's people."[80]

As a result of the command of Moses, the "Israelites captured the Midianite women and children and took all the

---

[78] Matthew 1:5; Ruth 4:21.
[79] Deuteronomy 20:17–18 (NIV).
[80] Numbers 31:1–2, 15–16 (NIV). See Numbers 25:11, for the incident of Peor and God's punishment on the children of Israel regarding their idol worship. See also Numbers 33:50–56 and Deuteronomy 7:1–2, 4–5 for a discussion regarding why God commanded that the inhabitants of the land were to be killed.

Midianite herds, flocks and goods as plunder. They burned all the towns where the Midianites had settled, as well as all their camps. They took all the plunder and spoils, including the people and animals."[81]

It is recorded that Moses commanded, "Now kill all the boys. And kill every woman who has slept with a man, but save for yourselves every girl who has never slept with a man. . . . The plunder remaining from the spoils that the soldiers took . . . [included] 32,000 women who had never slept with a man."[82]

The Law of Moses was harsh—kill all except the virgins and take them as spoils of war. But behind the command was mercy and the justice that the innocent shall not be punished with the guilty.

The Midianites and Moabites and others that God commanded to be destroyed practiced various types of abominations and idol worship and human sacrifices. God's justice required that such evil be answered with death and be wiped off the face of the earth. God also commanded them to be destroyed because they had enticed 24,000 of the children of Israel to indulge in the abominations at Peor. As for the young women, Moses commanded that they be spared because they were too young to have participated in the abominations, so it would have been unjust for them to be punished with death.

Even in war in which His armies laid waste to entire cities, God's justice demanded mercy in a land in which mercy and justice was not known. Dante told his men as they left to conquer new lands, "Consider ye the seed from which ye sprang; Ye were not made to live like unto brutes, But for pursuit of virtue and of knowledge."[83]

Similarly God commanded that His people, even in war, were not to act as brutes, and they were to care for the weak

---

[81] Numbers 31:9–11.

[82] Numbers 31:17–18, 32, 35.

[83] Dante Alighieri, *The Divine Comedy* Inferno Canto at XXVI (1320).

that fell into their hands. As a general law of war, God commanded:

> *When you go out to war against your enemies, and*
> *the Lord your God delivers them into your hand,*
> *and you take them captive, and you see among the*
> *captives a beautiful woman, and desire her and*
> *would take her for your wife, then you shall bring*
> *her home to your house, and she shall shave her*
> *head and trim her nails. She shall put off the*
> *clothes of her captivity, remain in your house, and*
> *mourn her father and her mother a full month; after*
> *that, you may go into her and be her husband and*
> *she shall be your wife. And it shall be, if you have*
> *no delight in her, then you shall set her free, but you*
> *certainly shall not sell her for money; you shall not*
> *treat her brutally, because you have humbled her.*[84]

God commanded that women captured in war were to be treated with mercy and integrated into the families of children of Israel. Ruth and Rahab were not anomalies.

The Law of Moses prevented the armies of Israel from indulging in the rape of the women of defeated enemies. This command was unheard of in the time of Moses, well into the time of the Greeks, the Roman Empire, and even in the not-so-recent twentieth century.

When the lowest and weakest of people—women captured by the enemy in time of war—fell under the authority of His people, God commanded that "you shall not mistreat her." God commanded further that *before* any soldier of the Israeli army has sex with a captured woman, who is defenseless, it was required of them to "take her as a wife . . . you shall bring her home to your house . . . and [she] shall remain in your house [and be allowed to] mourn her father and mother a full month." Consider the mercy and justice behind the rules of conquest that God had commanded.

---

[84] Deuteronomy 21:10–14.

First, God commanded that His people shall not commit rape in time of war. This is why it was and is known in the history of Israel and Judeo-Christian nations to this day that their armies do not commit rape, gang rape, or mass rape as a tool of war upon conquered cities as a regular lawful practice. It is from this tradition that in the modern world, armies that commit rape in times of war are considered war criminals. This is what separated the Russian, German, and Japanese armies from the British and American armies in World War II.

Second, God commanded that the weak and helpless shall be protected, not abused—"you shall not treat her brutally."

Third, consider what occurred during that month. In those days, the prime women who were carried away as captives would have been young women of childbearing age—anywhere from sixteen to eighteen—and younger. In other words, they were young girls who were still attached to and cared for by their parents, who had just been killed in war.

The soldier of Israel who carried off a young girl in war would hear this poor child cry all day and night for her dead family in fear of what would be done to her. He would feed and clothe her as she cried in terror before his eyes and in the presence of his family. Put simply, in that month, the hardened soldier of Israel would soften, and he would bond to her. Under his kind hand, she would see that she would be cared for and would not be raped, nor would she be sold into slavery to be raped. Under this mercy, she would bond to him. They would be reconciled. As David wrote, behind the harshness of God's law, there are wonders in His law.

Lastly, if the bonding did not occur, the soldier in the army of God was not permitted to sell a captured woman as a slave, an unheard of practice. God commanded, "you shall let her go wherever she wishes" because God's justice said, this is required, "because you have humbled her."

Ruth and Rahab would testify, as Sarah and Rebekah would before them,[85] that God acts in the affairs of men to protect the helpless. God protects the weak and commanded His people to do so because God's justice is very sensitive to the treatment of those who are weak, alone, and totally without physical protection in the world.

To summarize God's commands to His people, He warned the children of Israel throughout the books of Exodus and Deuteronomy:

> *Do not take advantage or mistreat those among you who are weak, helpless, and without protection, for if you mistreat them and as they will cry out to Me, I will hear them from heaven, and I will kill you in My righteous anger to rescue them, just as I killed the Egyptians and rescued you from their evil when you were slaves.*

---

[85] In Genesis, it is recorded how God rescued Sarah twice, first from the harem of the Egyptian King and then from the harem of King Abimelech (Genesis 12:15, 17–20). It also recorded how He protected Rebekah from the desires of the same King Abimelech and the Philistines (Genesis 26:7–11).

4.

In Your Courts of Law: You Shall Not Oppress the Stranger, for You Were Strangers in Egypt,[1] and You Shall Not Use Unjust Scales at Your Gates[2]

After four-hundred years of slavery and living in Egypt and being shaped by Egyptian culture, God wanted to make His chosen nation—the children of Abraham—a separate people. The purpose of the Law of Moses was to take Egypt out of the children of Israel. The Law of Moses also established a judicial system that has provided the foundation for Judeo-Christian concepts of justice and criminal justice.[3]

The Judeo-Christian Western tradition received from the Law of Moses the following concepts:

- proportionality in punishment,

- the right to appeal,

- distinctions between crimes,

- rules of evidence,

- the requirement that judges are to rule without partiality,

---

[1] Exodus 22:21.
[2] Leviticus 19:34–35.
[3] Arthur H. Garrison, *The Traditions and History of the Meaning of the Rule of Law,* 611–13; Arthur H. Garrison, *The Rule of Law and the Rise of Control of Executive Power,* 316–17, 320–21.

- the right to sanctuary,

- retribution (righteous vengeance for evil inflicted on the weak or disobedience of the law under God),

- incarceration (banishment) from society,

- parole and ability to return to society,

- sanctuary cities,

- distinctions of murder and theft,

- the requirement that criminal law must be written, as well as

- the principle that the law must be obeyed.

These principles, among others, are all written in the Books of Exodus, Leviticus, Deuteronomy, and Numbers.

The Law of Moses established the four concepts of punishment: retribution (revenge), incapacitation (preventing repeat offenses), incarceration (banishment), and rehabilitation (restoring the accused back into society). Justice under God and under the New Testament reflected the full manifestation of the fourth concept of punishment, rehabilitation (repentance and change), as well as the concept of restoration (repairing relationships).

When Moses brought six-hundred-thousand men and their families out of Egypt[4] with the plunder of gold and silver from the Egyptians[5] and in perfect health,[6] the practical issue of governance presented itself. Moses had brought out a population the size of a city, and they had to be governed to

---

[4] Exodus 12:37–38 ("Then the children of Israel journeyed from Rameses to Succoth, about six hundred thousand men on foot, besides children. A mixed multitude went up with them also, and flocks and herds—a great deal of livestock."). Two years later their number in the wilderness of the Sinai was 603,550 (Exodus 1:46) not counting the tribe of Levi who numbered 7,500 (Numbers 1:1, 46; 3:22).

[5] Exodus 12:36.

[6] Psalm 105:37 ("He also brought them out with silver and gold, and there was none feeble among His tribes.")

prevent crime and injustice. The Lord provided Moses with criminal, civil, Levitical, and ceremonial laws to govern the people.

The laws to govern the daily lives of the Jews began with the Ten Commandments. The first four commandments[7] govern how the Jews were to relate to their God. The third commandment prohibited taking the name of Lord and using it to commit fraud.[8] The fifth commandment, "Honor thy mother and father," governed how children should relate to their parents both when they are young and when their parents are old.[9] Of the remaining five commandments, which govern how the Jews were to relate to each other, the sixth, eighth, and ninth are criminal statutes. These prohibited murder, theft, and perjury.[10] The Ten Commandments were followed by more than six hundred laws, policies, procedures, and punishments recorded in Exodus, Leviticus, Numbers, and Deuteronomy.

To the generation who would cross over the Jordan, the generation after those who were brought out from Egypt, Moses gave twelve laws which if broken would bring a curse.[11] The first two reflected the original second and fifth commandments. The fifth, third, seventh, eighth, tenth, and eleventh were criminal statutes. These statutes were against obstruction of justice, property theft, and bestiality, as well as incest, assault, and bribery, respectively.[12] The fourth, sixth, ninth, and twelfth reflected laws governing family relationships and obedience to the laws of God.

---

[7] Have no Gods before me, no engraved images, no false use of the name of the Lord God, and remember the Sabbath day as Holy (Exodus 20:3–8).

[8] Compare Leviticus 19:11–12 with Exodus 20:7.

[9] Exodus 20:12.

[10] Exodus 20:13–16. The tenth commandment, you shall not covet what belongs to others, provides an explanation for why the sins prohibited by the sixth, seventh, eighth, and ninth occur. Jealousy causes people to kill, cheat, steal, and lie to get what they do not have from others who have.

[11] Deuteronomy 27:15–26.

[12] Deuteronomy 27:19, 21, 22, 25.

From Exodus 21 through the Books of Leviticus, Numbers, and Deuteronomy, the Law of Moses and the commands of God made clear that God required justice and provided criminal statutes to govern the nation.

In Exodus 21, the crimes of first- and second-degree manslaughter, murder, kidnapping, criminal negligent homicide, and simple assault are defined, and the punishment was to be proportional to the injury caused by a criminal act.[13] The Law famously made clear, "if any harm follows, then you shall give life for life, eye for eye, tooth for tooth, hand for hand, foot for foot, burn for burn, wound for wound, stripe for stripe."[14] "If a man causes disfigurement of his neighbor, as he has done, so shall it be done to him—fracture for fracture, eye for eye, tooth for tooth; as he has caused disfigurement of a man, so shall it be done to him."[15]

Under the Third Commandment, God commanded, "You shall not take the name of the Lord your God in vain, for the Lord will not hold him guiltless who takes His name in vain."[16]

God instructed that the use of His name falsely in contracts was a crime. When a deal was made, each party would swear by the name of God that they would comply with the deal. It was through using the name of God that trust in contracts and financial dealing could be made. Thus, God commanded that the use of His name and then failure to comply was using His name in vain.

Financial crimes of fraud as well as perjury required restitution to the victim and the priest as an offering for the forgiveness of God. Financial crimes included failure to honor financial contracts, perjury, fraud, extortion, and financial theft. Such crimes required restitution and restoration:

And the Lord spoke to Moses, saying: "If a person sins and commits a trespass against the Lord by

---

13 Exodus 21:12–36.
14 Exodus 21:23–25.
15 Leviticus 24:19–20.
16 Exodus 20:7.

lying to his neighbor about what was delivered to him for safekeeping, or about a pledge, or about a robbery, or if he has extorted from his neighbor, or if he has found what was lost and lies concerning it, and swears falsely—in any one of these things that a man may do in which he sins: then it shall be, because he has sinned and is guilty, that he shall restore what he has stolen, or the thing which he has extorted, or what was delivered to him for safekeeping, or the lost thing which he found, or all that about which he has sworn falsely. He shall restore its full value, add one-fifth more to it, and give it to whomever it belongs, on the day of his trespass offering. And he shall bring his trespass offering to the Lord, a ram without blemish from the flock, with your valuation, as a trespass offering, to the priest. So the priest shall make atonement for him before the Lord, and he shall be forgiven for any one of these things that he may have done in which he trespasses."[17]

In Exodus 22, the punishment for theft is restitution, and if deadly force is used to repel the thief, the concept of self-defense is permitted when a nighttime burglar is killed.[18] The Law made a distinction between burglary and robbery. The chapter makes clear that burglary during the day does not allow the same defense.[19]

In the next chapter, the Law of Moses makes clear that under the Law the stranger shall not be oppressed, and later it is written that in the courts, "You shall not circulate a false report . . . . [nor] show partiality to a poor man in his dispute. . . . You shall not pervert the judgment of your poor in his dispute."[20]

In Leviticus, the Law establishes the distinction between crimes of omission and commission, applies different sanc-

---

[17] Leviticus 6:1–7.
[18] Exodus 22:1–2.
[19] Exodus 22:3.
[20] Exodus 23:1, 3, 6, 9.

tions for each,[21] and criminalizes the failure to report fraud or taking a false oath.[22] In the same book, the sanction for unintentional violation of the law was financial restitution,[23] and ignorance of the law is no defense. "If a person sins, and commits any of these things which are forbidden to be done by the commandments of the Lord, though he does not know it, yet he is guilty and shall bear his iniquity."[24]

But for the person who breaks the law intentionally, the sanction was banishment.[25] In cases of perjury, "if the witness is a false witness, who has testified falsely against his brother, then you shall do to him as he thought to have done to his brother."[26]

God made clear that the evil of a crime begins in the heart: "You shall not hate your brother in your heart...not bear any grudge."[27] Through this command God warned that crime begins with unkind emotions and justifications for evil—hatred and holding a grudge. From this concept, motive ("You shall not covet") is made distinct from *mens rea* and *actus reus*.

God commanded that the criminal law would recognize distinctions between intentional and unintentional crimes, and all laws shall apply equally to all. "You shall have one law for him who sins unintentionally, whether he is native-born among the Israelites or a stranger who is living among them as a resident alien."[28] Equality before the law was a significant requirement under the Law of Moses. It was commanded:

---

[21] Leviticus 4:22–28. See also Numbers 35:16–29.
[22] Leviticus 5:1.
[23] Numbers 15:22–29.
[24] Leviticus 5:17.
[25] Numbers 15:30–31.
[26] Deuteronomy 19:18–19.
[27] Leviticus 19:17–18.
[28] Numbers 15:29 (AMP); "Ye shall have one law for him that sinneth through ignorance, both for him that is born among the children of Israel, and for the stranger that sojourneth among them." Numbers 15:29 (KJV).

You shall do no injustice in judgment. You shall not be partial to the poor, nor honor the person of the mighty. In righteousness, you shall judge your neighbor. You shall not go about as a talebearer among your people; nor shall you take a stand against the life of your neighbor: I am the Lord.[29]

You shall have the same law for the stranger and for one from your own country; for I am the Lord your God.[30]

Then I commanded your judges at that time, saying, Hear the cases between your brethren, and judge righteously between a man and his brother or the stranger who is with him. You shall not show partiality in judgment; you shall hear the small as well as the great; you shall not be afraid in any man's presence, for the judgment is God's.[31]

You shall appoint judges and officers . . . and they shall judge the people with just judgment. You shall not pervert justice; you shall not show partiality, nor take a bribe, for a bribe blinds the eyes of the wise and twists the words of the righteous.[32]

From the days of Moses to the modern legal system in the West, these principles are foundational in the operation of the judicial system.

Under Moses, the judicial system had a hierarchy in which appeals from a judicial judgment of disputes were brought from smaller judicial officers to higher ones to Moses himself and then to God.[33] As written in Exodus, Moses established the qualifications for a judge. Moses commanded that those who apply law and justice and settle disputes were to be "able men, such as fear God, men of truth, hating cov-

---

[29] Leviticus 19:15–16.
[30] Leviticus 24:22.
[31] Deuteronomy 1:16–17 (internal quotation marks omitted).
[32] Deuteronomy 16:18–19.
[33] Exodus 18:21–23.

etousness," and such men were to judge disputes and apply the Law so that justice would prevail.[34]

These principles are reflected in the judicial oath required under federal law[35] and in Western tradition,[36] as Justice Stephen Breyer noted: "Justice shall not be sold nor shall it be denied . . . that's at least 800 years old."[37]

Under Moses, not only was justice to be done, but it was done under the name of God. In modern times, justice is done in the name of the State to defend the value of life. In the courts of justice, the law is to be applied with impartiality, which has formed the truism that no one is above the law nor below it, and all are equal before the law.

---

[34] Exodus 18:21.

[35] The following is the judicial oath required for all federal judicial officers:
"Each Justice or judge of the United States shall take the following oath or affirmation before performing the duties of his office:
"I,___ _, do solemnly swear (or affirm) that I will administer Justice without respect to persons, and do equal right to the poor and to the rich, and that I will faithfully and impartially discharge and perform all the duties incumbent upon me as ___ under the Constitution and laws of the United States. So help me God." 28 U.S.C. § 453 (2012).

[36] As the *Magna Carta* (1215) makes clear,
38. No bailiff for the future shall, upon his own unsupported complaint, put anyone to his "law", without credible witnesses brought for this purposes.
39. No freemen shall be taken or imprisoned or disseised [dispossessed or deprived] or exiled or in any way destroyed, nor will we go upon him nor send upon him, except by the lawful judgment of his peers or by the law of the land.
40. To no one will we sell, to no one will we refuse or delay, right or Justice.

[37] Transcript of Oral Argument at 46, *Williams-Yulee v. Florida Bar*, 135 S. Ct. 1656 (2015) (No. 131499) (citing clause 40 of the Magna Carta). In this case, the United States Supreme Court held that although judges can be elected; the rules of the judicial canon and tradition to impart justice with impartiality can govern how judges finance their elections. See *Williams-Yulee v. Florida Bar*, 135 S. Ct 1656, 1666 (2015). Public confidence in the judiciary to impart justice occurs when justice is not only done but when it is perceived to be done. *Rex v. Sussex Justices* (1924) 1 K.B. 256, 259.

In the movie *The Judge*, the prosecutor justified why he
was prosecuting a beloved judge who had killed an incorrigible child murderer, who mocked the judge by threatening
to desecrate the graves of his victim and the judge's wife:

> *I have one simple belief. That the law is the only
> thing capable of making people equal. You may
> think Mark Blackwell was white trash, and he may
> very well have been, but in the eyes of the [law and
> thus the] state, his life matters.*[38]

Under the law, all people matter and have a right to justice.

As Moses made clear, justice is not only a reflection of
God, but justice is done in the name of God. Moses commanded that justice was to be imposed equally and they were
to remember when they were slaves and the law of Egypt
provided no protection to them and justice was denied.

Under the Law of Moses, it was to be known that in Israel
the people do not oppress the stranger and that the Law is
applied to the brother and stranger alike.

Whenever God commanded that the stranger and the weak
were not to be abused, He concluded the command with the
phrases, "you were strangers in the land of Egypt"[39] or "you
shall remember that you were a slave in the land of Egypt;
therefore, I command you to do this thing."[40]

The Law commanded that the rule of law was to govern all
disputes, and the judgment of God through the priests and
judges was final. In addition, the Law of Moses instituted the
principle of public trials and public punishment, both to cre-
ate deterrence and to establish that no punishment would be
implemented beyond what the Law required:

> *If there is a dispute between men, and they come to
> court, that the judges may judge them, and they jus-*

---

[38] *The Judge*, directed by David Dobkin, written by Nick Schenk, Bill
Dubuque, and David Dobkin, featuring Robert Downey, Jr., Robert
Duvall, and Vera Farmiga (Burbank, CA: Warner Bros., 2014).

[39] Exodus 22:21; 23:9; Leviticus 19:34; Deuteronomy 10:19; 24:18.

[40] Deuteronomy 24:22.

*tify the righteous and condemn the wicked, then it
shall be, if the wicked man deserves to be beaten,
that the judge will cause him to lie down and be
beaten in his presence, according to his guilt, with a
certain number of blows. Forty blows he may give
him and no more, lest he should exceed this and
beat him with many blows above these, and your
brother be humiliated in your sight.[41]*

To maintain justice in the courts of His people, God required rules of evidence in the courts, which included the requirement that in a death penalty case, more than one witness to the killing was required to prove guilt.[42] To secure a conviction on any charge, "one witness shall not rise against a man concerning any iniquity or any sin that he commits; by the mouth of two or three witnesses the matter shall be established."[43]

Both laws of evidence, among many other laws and rules of evidence, were broken at the trial of Jesus before the Sanhedrin.[44] The illegality of the trial of Jesus included, conspiracy and bribery between Judas and the high priest to lodge a false charge in open court,[45] arrest of Jesus without a warrant,[46] assault of a prisoner in open court,[47] conducting a

---

[41] Deuteronomy 25:1–3.

[42] See Numbers 35:30 (NKJV); Deuteronomy 17:6.

[43] Deuteronomy 19:15.

[44] See, Laurna L. Berg, *The Illegalities of Jesus' Religious and Civil Trials.* Bibliotheca Sacra-Dallas (2004): 330-342; John Evan Richards and S. Srinivasa Aiyar. *The Illegality of the Trial of Jesus: The Legality of the Trial of Jesus.* Platt & Peck Company (1915); Hala Khoury-Bisharat and Rinat Kitai-Sangero. *The Silence of Jesus and Its Significance for the Accused.* Tulsa L. Rev. 55 (2019): 443; Alexander S. Bacon, *The Illegal Trial of Christ* Law & Banker & S. Bench & B. Rev. 11 (1918): 145; F. L. Grant *The People of Israel vs. Jesus of Nazareth.* In Dicta, vol. 6, p. 17. 1928.

[45] Matthew 26:14–15; Mark 14:1, 10–11; Luke 22:1–4; John 13:2.

[46] Matthew 26:47; Mark 14:43; Luke 47:47, 52; John 18:2–3, 12.

[47] Luke 22:63–65; John 18:22–24.

capital punishment trial[48] in the dark,[49] introduction of perjury as evidence,[50] conviction of blasphemy without witnesses,[51] and assault of a prisoner to the point of disfigurement[52] in open court.[53]

Upon being turned over to Pilate for execution, Jesus said, "the one who delivered Me to you has the greater sin"[54] for Pilate knew Jesus was innocent.[55] His conviction occurred because the priests were jealous of Him and they raised up a mob in Pilate's court.[56] Jesus was convicted by the Sanhedrin and Pilate unjustly with a mob demanding that a murderer be released.

The trial of Jesus offers proof that when the law and legal process are perverted and the court is intimidated, the result is always a miscarriage of justice. A criminal trial without the rule of law is justice in the hand of the mob. When justice is in the hand of the mob, Barabbas always goes free.

Adherence to the law in a trial is key to the achievement of justice. As the Law of Moses commanded: "Judges. . . shall not pervert justice...shall not...bribe, for a bribe...twists the words of the righteous.[57] From this, western tradition and American law requires procedural due process to govern the

[48] Matthew 26:57, 59.
[49] Matthew 26:20, 25; Mark 14:17. Luke's account implies that they tried him in the early morning not at night (Luke 22:66–70). John's account supports the account of the trial occurring at night when Jesus tells Peter before rooster crows he will deny him three times. Which implies that the denial occurs before the morning since that is when roosters crow (John 13:38).
[50] Matthew 26:59–62; Mark 14:55–59.
[51] Matthew 26: 65–66; Mark 14:64; Luke 22:71.
[52] Isaiah 50: 6 ("I gave My back to those who struck Me, And My cheeks to those who plucked out the beard; I did not hide My face from shame and spitting.").
[53] Matthew 26: 67 ("Then they spat in His face and beat Him; and others struck Him with the palms of their hands"); Mark 14:65. Luke's account implies that guards assaulted Jesus before his trial (Luke 22:63–65).
[54] John 19:11.
[55] Luke 23:4.
[56] Matthew 27:18,20–26.
[57] Deuteronomy 16:18–19.

rules of criminal trials as well as requiring substantive due process to make sure that the rules are fair and just before the bar of justice.

The Lord also made provisions for those who were banished and those who sought escape from the punishment of manslaughter. Even under the harshness of the Law of Moses, a method of restitution and reconciliation was provided. The edge of the Law was blunted by the grace of mercy.

The Law of Moses commanded the children of Israel, when they crossed over the Jordan, "You shall appoint cities to be cities of refuge for you, that the manslayer who kills any person accidentally may flee there. They shall be cities of refuge for you from the avenger, that the manslayer may not die until he stands before the congregation in judgment."[58] The purpose of the sanctuary city was to protect the manslayer from the anger of the family of the person who was killed.[59]

The Law of Moses provided distinctions between types of murder and the sanctions applied. Involuntary manslaughter could result in sanctuary, but intentional murder was sanctioned with the death penalty. Although God commanded that the three sanctuary cities be built to protect the manslayer, the Law required that a person who commits intentional murder and "flees to one of these cities, then the elders of his city shall send and bring him from there, and deliver him over to the hand of the avenger of blood, that he may die. Your eye shall not pity him, but you shall put away the guilt of innocent blood from Israel, that it may go well with you."[60]

The sanctuary law allowed for a person to be safe from punishment in the city of refuge; he would be allowed to return after the life of the high priest, at the time of the man-

[58] Numbers 35:11–12.
[59] Deuteronomy 19:6 ("Lest the avenger of blood, while his anger is hot, pursue the manslayer and overtake him, because the way is long, and kill him, though he was not deserving of death.").
[60] Deuteronomy 19:2, 11–13.

slaughter, had ended without fear of death due to the killing.[61] The sanctuary law provided for incarceration, determinate/mandatory sentencing, and re-entry after the completion of the imposed sentence.

---

[61] Numbers 35:26–28.

5.

I Am God and Next to Me There Is No Other God;[1] You Are in My Hand[2] and Cannot Be Removed,[3] for I Am God and I Cannot Lie[4]

---

[1] See Deuteronomy 4:35, 39; 6:4; 2 Samuel 7:22; 2 Kings 5:15; Isaiah 42:8; 43:10–11; 44:6; 24; 45:5–6; 21–22; 48:12; Hosea 13:4; Mark 12:29–34; 1 Corinthians 8:4–6; 1 Timothy 2:5; Revelation 1:8; 22:13; see also Psalm 90:2; Malachi 3:6 ("For I am the Lord, I do not change.").

[2] Isaiah 41:13 ("For I, the Lord your God, will hold your right hand, Saying to you, 'Fear not, I will help you'") and Isaiah 49:15–16 ("Can a woman forget her nursing child, and not have compassion on the son of her womb? Surely they may forget, yet I will not forget you. See, I have inscribed you on the palms of My hands."). As David wrote: "Where can I go from Your Spirit? Or where can I flee from Your presence? If I ascend into heaven, You are there; If I make my bed in hell, behold, You are there. If I take the wings of the morning, And dwell in the uttermost parts of the sea, Even there Your hand shall lead me, And Your right hand shall hold me" (Psalm 139:7–10). Daniel reminded the King that God is mighty and in His "hand are your life-breath and all your ways." Daniel 5:23 (NASB).

[3] Jesus said, "My sheep hear My voice, and I know them, and they follow Me. And I give them eternal life, and they shall never perish; neither shall anyone snatch them out of My hand. My Father, who has given them to Me, is greater than all; and no one is able to snatch them out of My Father's hand. I and My Father are one" (John 10:27–30). See also Deuteronomy 32:39 ("Now see that I, even I, am He, And there is no God besides Me; I kill and I make alive; I wound and I heal; Nor is there any who can deliver from My hand.") and Isaiah 43:13 ("And there is no one who can deliver out of My hand.").

[4] Numbers 23:19 ("God is not a man, that He should lie."); see also John 14:6 ("I am the way, the truth, and the life."); 1 Peter 2:22 ("Nor was deceit found in His mouth") (citing Isaiah 53:9).

What is justice? On one level, Akiva is correct that justice is an abstraction. Justice is a concept of what ought and ought not to be. It does have a subjective narrative to its definition.

But Akiva was wrong that justice is devoid of objective meaning. The true operation and implementation of justice can be objectively defined. When justice occurs it is observed, "the wilderness will become a fertile field, and the fertile field will yield bountiful crops [and] righteousness will bring peace...quietness and confidence forever [and] people will live in safety, quietly at home. They will be at rest."[5]

Justice has actual meaning on the governmental level. Justice is an action and a goal to be achieved, and it can be objectively measured.

Justice begins with the law and its enforcement, but it is fully achieved by the application of mercy and grace. The definition of justice is defined by how God Himself, as reflected in the Bible, seeks mercy and gives grace in the face of the harshness of the Law, while using the Law to define right and wrong.

The meaning of law and justice, in the Western Judeo-Christian tradition, begins with the truism that there is a God, and He is just. The tradition begins with the proposition that God sees and cares about the actions of men. He is the final authority to be appealed to in matters of right and wrong and what is just in a world governed by men.

Justice and the law are very specific and definable concepts. Justice is defined by protecting widows and orphans and despising unequal scales of judgment. Justice executes punishment upon those who do evil, and requires those who govern to defend and protect those who are small and weak in the face of men with power.

Justice equalizes inequity. The law governs behavior, defines relationships, and requires obedience. Justice is a broader concept and seeks to define a society and elevate it

---

[5]   Isaiah 32:15-18 (NLT).

beyond the need for raw control to a level of being just and justly governed.

Justice tempers the sharp and cold edge of the law and governs the hands of those who hold the power of the law over the heads of men. This is the Judeo-Christian tradition that defines both law and justice, as well as the distinctions between the two.

The law entails distinctions and classifications, and the enforcement of each. The law is not about fairness in outcome. The law is about the enforcement of order and providing security. The law is written in stone. The law is about what is required in a situation. The law is about the application of consequences. The law is what the law does.

The law does not guarantee justice or even require justice. The law provides definitions of behavior, distinctions within types of behavior, expectations of behavior, and enforces norms of behavior. The law also defines and separates people and classes of people. The law establishes order and safety, which allows the higher principles and goals of justice to occur.

Nations are considered stable when they are governed by the law and not the whims of men. In other words, nations are considered stable when rule of law governs, which is when the law is over all including government.

Justice is a much broader concept. Justice allows for mercy and release from the requirements of the law. Justice is a societal, as well as an individual, objective. Justice encompasses both the procedure of the application of the law and the substantive outcome of the application of positive law. The former is about what is required, but the latter includes normative concepts of fair outcomes. Justice includes how a law is passed, why a law is passed, and whether the law is, as Moses commanded, equally applied to brother and stranger.

Nations are considered just when outcomes are perceived as right and fair. Justice is a system of recognizing what is right and what is wrong in society and in individual behavior.

Justice provides protection as well as security from evil under the letter of the law. Justice utilizes the law to maintain security, but justice is about security and order, tempered by grace and mercy. Justice provides safety and security from the sharp edges of the requirements of the law. It includes the propositions about what is true and what is virtuous, and provides the foundation for the concept of the rule of law. "There can be no virtue without freedom and no peace without justice."[6] "There can be no rule of law, however, unless citizens and especially leaders are convinced that there is no freedom without truth."[7] The rule of law is what shields a society from the encroachment of tyranny under the guise of order.[8]

While the law is what law does and requires or obligates, justice is what justice seeks. Concurrently, while it is true that justice is broader in scope than her daughter, the law, the achievement of justice begins with the law. "[T]he end of law is not to abolish or restrain, but to preserve and enlarge freedom…where there is no law, there is no freedom: for liberty… cannot be, where there is no law."[9]

John Locke teaches that the law controls the evil nature of man's behavior, so man can have the freedom to enjoy his

---

6   Quote attributed to Frederick Douglass. Yale University Library, Frederick Douglass autograph, 1859 Document 8 x 5.

7   Post-Synodal Apostolic Exhortation Ecclesia in America of the Holy Father John Paul II (January 22, 1999) at https://www.vatican.va/content/john-paul-ii/en/apost_exhortations/documents/hf_jp-ii_exh_22011999_ecclesia-in-america.html.

8   See, Robert John Araujo, *John Paul II and the Rule of Law: Bringing Order to International Disorder.* J. Cath. Leg. Stud. 45 (2006): 293; Arthur H. Garrison, *The Traditions and History of the Meaning of the Rule of Law*, 12 Geo. J.L. & Pub. Pol'y 565, 565 (2014); Arthur H. Garrison, *The Rule of Law and the Rise of Control of Executive Power*, 18 Tex. Rev. L. & Pol. 303, 304 (2014); Allen W. West, *President's Message-The Constitution Liberates Us: The Rule of Law and How It Enables Equal Protection, Justice, and an Enduring Freedom for All* Federal Bar Association Annual Meeting August 9, 2021, at https://www.fedbar.org/blog/presidents-message-the-constitution-liberates-us/.

9   John Locke, *Two Treatises of Government* (1689) at 234.

lawful desires. While justice includes higher concepts of right and wrong, the law provides order so that freedom can be maintained. While law and justice are not the same because they serve different interests and goals, both work in tandem. Justice is the goal of society, while the law is a tool of order for society. The Law, as Moses and Joshua asserted, is written on stone to be a witness against the acts of man,[10] and to define what is evil;[11] but justice is written on the heart of man[12] for his liberty and freedom.

While the law is a positivist concept, justice is both a normative concept—subjective and value/morality oriented—and a positivist concept—objective, testable, and fact oriented. Justice involves concepts of fairness, rightness, and results that are both perceived as good and reasonable and achieve fair outcomes.

Justice involves the higher levels of considerations of what ought to be in a situation. Justice involves the inward heart of a man, not only his outward behavior. As the Bible defines these terms, justice is something to be sought and achieved, while the law is something to be guided by.

If God governs heaven with justice, mankind on earth is required to do the same. Jesus prayed, "Your will be done on earth as it is done in heaven."[13] The source of the need for justice, as well as her daughter, the law, comes from the nature of God Himself. The entire world is in His hands, and all those who rule are in His hands. Those who rule are to be held to a higher standard and their positions require, *per se*, a level of temperance and righteousness. Solomon records the words of a mother of a king who told her son:

> *It is not for kings, O Lemuel, it is not for kings to drink wine, nor for princes intoxicating drink; lest they drink and forget the law, and pervert the justice of all the afflicted. . . . Open your mouth for the*

---

10 Exodus 24:12-18; Joshua 24:27.
11 Romans 4:15.
12 Ezekiel 11:19; Ezekiel 36:26; Jeremiah 31:33; Hebrews 8:10.
13 Matthew 6:10.

speechless, in the cause of all who are appointed to die. Open your mouth, judge righteously, and plead the cause of the poor and needy.[14]

The idea that the role of government is to enforce the distinction between right and wrong and the need for justice defines the Judeo-Christian tradition. As John Locke has been paraphrased, "without the law there can be no freedom, and without justice, there can be no law."[15] As inscribed on the walls of the U.S. Department of Justice building, "Justice is founded in the rights bestowed by nature upon man. Liberty is maintained in security of justice" and inscribed over the door of the U.S. Supreme Court, "Equal Justice Under Law." As the U.S. Pledge of Allegiance concludes, it is not law and order that form the foundation of American values, but it is "one Nation under God, indivisible, with liberty and justice for all."

The western tradition of justice being the higher interest of the courts is inscribed over the door of the 1907 Old Bailey Courthouse in England. It reads, "Defend the children of the poor and punish the wrongdoer." The command of the inscription is supported by three statues—the first being *Fortitude*, the second being the *Recording Angel*, and the third being *Truth*.

The Scriptures make clear that God loves justice,[16] that He is a God of justice,[17] that He is "merciful and gracious, long-suffering, and abounding in goodness and truth, keeping mercy for thousands, forgiving iniquity and transgression."[18]

---

[14] Proverbs 31:4–5, 8–9.

[15] NBC Television Series Law & Order (Season 8, Episode 5), *Nullification* (Nov 5, 1997). See discussion, Arthur H. Garrison, *The Traditions and History of the Meaning of the Rule of Law*, 12 Geo. J.L. & Pub. Pol'y 565 (2014).

[16] See Isaiah 61:8; Psalm 33:5; see also Isaiah 30:18; Deuteronomy 32:4.

[17] See Isaiah 30:18, 66:24; Job 34:12; Psalm 9:7–8, 140:12; Revelation 20:12–13.

[18] Exodus 34:6–7.

While the law brings death and separation,[19] God's justice seeks restoration through the application of grace and mercy: "For the law was given through Moses, but grace and truth came through Jesus Christ."[20] Where the law abounds, grace and mercy still more abound.[21]

The answer to what justice is, how it is defined, and why justice is something to be done, can be summarized as follows (several verses paraphrased):

> *God is justice and justice is defined by grace, mercy, and reconciliation which is to be applied to and between and among all mankind because God says, I Am the Lord who does justice, for I Am your God who delivered you from Egypt and you shall not oppress because you were once a slave and were delivered from oppression by My hand.*[22]

Justice defends the repentant in the face of arrogant self-righteousness;[23] justice provides mercy for the condemned;[24] justice commutes the sentence of the guilty;[25] justice speaks for the weak and advocates for the powerless and defenseless;[26] justice consoles the sick and visits those in prison;[27] justice speaks the truth tempered by humility;[28] justice res-

---

[19] See 1 Corinthians 15:56; 2 Corinthians 3:7–8; Hebrews 10:1; Colossians 2:16; Galatians 2:16; 3:21–22; Romans 3:20; 1 Timothy 1:8–9; James 2:10.

[20] John 1:17.

[21] Romans 5:20.

[22] See Genesis 18:19; Deuteronomy 5:6; Exodus 23:9; Micah 6:8; Psalms 96:10, 13.

[23] The prostitute and her repentance is defended in the face of the Pharisees (Luke 7:43–50).

[24] The thief on the cross (Luke 23:40–43).

[25] The women caught in adultery, whose death sentence was commuted (John 8:1–11).

[26] God commands those is power to plead for the poor and the needy and speak for those who are speechless (Proverbs 31:8–9).

[27] See Isaiah 42:7; Matthew 25:35–40.

[28] See Colossians 4:6; Micah 6:8; Corinthians 16:4.

cues the abandoned and captive;[29] justice condemns the false use of power;[30] and justice speaks the truth in the face of unjust punishment.[31]

---

[29] God told King Abimelech that He would kill him because he stole an honest man's wife. God sent the Prophet Nathan to confront King David for the murder of Uriah and stealing his wife Bathsheba (Genesis 20:3–6; 2 Samuel 12:1–15).

[30] Jesus accuses the religious leaders of hypocrisy and watering down the Law of God for their own purposes and pleasures of power (Matthew 23:13–37) and Stephen accuses the religious leaders of knowing the truth of God, but deciding to reject it as generations of leaders before them did the same, but prayed for God to forgive them as they stoned him to death for his preaching and accusations (Acts 7:51–60).

[31] For the story of the arrests and beatings of Paul and Silas, see Acts 16:16–24. For the story of the arrests and beatings of Peter and John, see Acts 4:18–19; 5:28–32; 40–41.

Conclusion

A story of justice.[1] The story goes that a young man, who was the son of a very rich man, would stop each day and speak to a homeless man. Over time, the homeless man became very fond of the young man. One day, the young man stopped coming. The homeless man asked about the young man, and he was told that the young man had died.

He knew that the father loved the young man. The homeless man drew a portrait of the young man and arranged to have it delivered to the father, along with the story of how the young man would visit him. The homeless man wanted the father to know how much his son had meant to him.

As the story goes, the father later died. Being a rich man, he had hundreds of paintings worth a small fortune. The homeless man heard that all the paintings, portraits, and other valuable drawings were being auctioned. The homeless man secured a suit and found a way into the auction. He wanted to see if the drawing that he had made for the father was open for sale. Indeed, the drawing was there among the valued art. The auction started with the sale of the drawing by the homeless man. The homeless man made a bid. No one else placed a bid, so the homeless man won the drawing.

After the sale, all the other buyers got ready to bid on the valuable artworks. However, the auctioneer said all the other paintings were sold. He explained that the father's will made

---

[1] A parable told by Dr. Ravi Zacharias on *The John Ankerberg Show*, *Ravi Zacharias Answers Questions from Europe*, Part 3 at https://www.youtube.com/watch?v=NEPrE57DlzA.

clear that whoever bought the drawing of his son got all the other valuable works of art with the purchase.

The law, like the drawing, has an obvious-but-finite value. Justice, like all the property of the father, is infinite but not completely self-defined. The meaning of justice begins with, but is not solely defined by, the value of the law.

About the Author

Dr. Arthur Garrison is a professor of Criminal Justice at Kutztown University and a member of the Enon Tabernacle Baptist Church, Philadelphia, Pennsylvania. Dr. Garrison has written books and articles on various topics including Western legal history and biblical hermeneutics and biblical worldview on faith, law, and justice.

If you feel generous and have a couple of minutes, please leave a review. It makes a significant difference for the author. Thank you in advance.

Visit the author's website at https://drarthurgarrison.com/

About the Publisher

Sulis International Press publishes select fiction and nonfiction in a variety of genres under four imprints: Riversong Books, Sulis Academic Press, Sulis Press, and Keledei Publications.

For more, visit the website at
https://sulisinternational.com

Subscribe to the newsletter at
https://sulisinternational.com/subscribe/

Follow on social media
https://www.facebook.com/SulisInternational
https://x.com/Sulis_Intl
https://www.pinterest.com/Sulis_Intl/
https://www.instagram.com/sulis_international/

www.ingramcontent.com/pod-product-compliance
Lightning Source LLC
Chambersburg PA
CBHW030943090426
42737CB00007B/521